Breakdown, Breakthrough

BREAKDOWN, BREAKTHROUGH

The Professional Woman's Guide
to Claiming a Life of
Passion, Power, and Purpose

✳ ✳ ✳

Kathy Caprino

Berrett–Koehler Publishers, Inc.
San Francisco
a BK Life book

Berrett-Koehler Publishers, Inc.
1333 Broadway, Suite 1000
Oakland, CA 94612-1921
Tel: (510) 817-2277   Fax: (510) 817-2278   www.bkconnection.com

Ordering Information
Quantity sales. Special discounts are available on quantity purchases by corporations, associations, and others. For details, contact the "Special Sales Department" at the Berrett-Koehler address above.
Individual sales. Berrett-Koehler publications are available through most bookstores.
They can also be ordered directly from Berrett-Koehler: Tel: (800) 929-2929; Fax: (802) 864-7626; www.bkconnection.com
Orders for college textbook/course adoption use. Please contact Berrett-Koehler: Tel: (800) 929-2929; Fax: (802) 864-7626.
Orders by U.S. trade bookstores and wholesalers. Please contact Ingram Publisher Services, Tel: (800) 509-4887; Fax: (800) 838-1149; E-mail: customer.service@ingrampublisherservices.com; or visit www.ingrampublisherservices.com/Ordering for details about electronic ordering.

Berrett-Koehler and the BK logo are registered trademarks of Berrett-Koehler Publishers, Inc.

Printed in the United States of America

Berrett-Koehler books are printed on long-lasting acid-free paper. When it is available, we choose paper that has been manufactured by environmentally responsible processes. These may include using trees grown in sustainable forests, incorporating recycled paper, minimizing chlorine in bleaching, or recycling the energy produced at the paper mill.

LIBRARY OF CONGRESS CATALOGING-IN-PUBLICATION DATA
Caprino, Kathy, 1960–
    Breakdown, breakthrough : the professional woman's guide to claiming a life of passion, power, and purpose / Kathy Caprino. — 1st ed.
        p. cm.
    Includes bibliographical references and index.
    ISBN 978-1-57675-559-4 (pbk. : alk. paper)
    1. Midlife crisis. 2. Middle-aged women—Psychology. 3. Women in the professions. I. Title.

BF724.65.M53C37 2008
155.6'6082—dc22   2008032706

First Edition
21   20   19   18   17   16   10   9   8   7   6   5   4   3   2

For Mom and Dad,
Thank you for encouraging me
to say yes! to myself, always.
I love you.

CONTENTS

Empowerment with Higher Self

PREFACE

yes is a world
& in this world of
yes live
(skilfully curled)
all worlds

E. E. CUMMINGS

After sixteen years in the workforce, I had achieved what many professional women dream of, but I was miserable. A corporate vice president with a lucrative and high-powered job, I was blessed with what seemed like a great career, a loving husband, two beautiful children, and a charming house in a quaint New England town. I had all the signs and symbols of "success" in life. I had it all. Or so it appeared, until I awakened suddenly at age 38 to a burning question. I asked myself over and over, *"Why am I so unhappy?"*

My family life had always been fulfilling and satisfying to me. I loved being a mother and wife, and I experienced these roles as enriching, filling life with meaning, joy, and satisfaction. But personal fulfillment has never been enough for me, for reasons that are deeply rooted in my experiences as a child and teen. Since I was 16, I have known that being an accomplished professional was something I deeply wanted, and having others view me this way was also important. I believed then (and still do) that developing the "chops" of working—building professional proficiency and forging the necessary skills, strengths, and talents to rise to new challenges and succeed in the workplace—adds a vital dimension to my life. I thought, too, that a career would guarantee that I could have something all my own to shape and mold—something no one could ever take away from me.

But in midlife all professional joy and satisfaction withered away, and my traumas at work began to "bleed" into my personal world. Strange, unsettling things were happening. My husband one day broke down in tears out of the blue and said, "I'm not sure I can take this anymore. You're just so angry and hostile all the time." I was shocked and hurt but realized, suddenly, that he was right. I had become addicted to taking out my intense work frustration and resentment on him.

I'd been suffering, too, from a serious chronic illness—a condition called tracheitis—which for four years hit me every four months or so without fail. It was debilitating, painful, frightening, and, in some inexplicable way, infuriating to me. I'd lose my voice completely and suffer from sharp, burning pain in the throat and chest. Fever would consume me, along with aches and exhaustion. Doctors couldn't find a cause or a cure. Due to all this sickness, I was constantly angry and resentful, and I felt depleted all the time. Functioning on every level became a chore. I knew something was very wrong, but I hadn't fully realized that things were truly falling apart and a "breakdown" was emerging.

I began to grapple with the all-important question I read somewhere, *"When I am 90 years old and looking back, what do I want to have accomplished, experienced, and given in this lifetime?"* My contemplation made me recognize I hadn't a clue what I wanted my life to stand for, or even the type of individual I would hold up as a role model. I did know, however, that I was drowning in a sea of wasted opportunities, and time was running out. I urgently longed to step away from feeling hurt at work, and hurting others. I looked everywhere for guidance—books, assessment tests, consultants, career coaches, mentors, colleagues, friends. But despite my many efforts, I remained stuck, unable to move forward in a meaningful way.

At the suggestion of a friend, I sought psychotherapy to help me get to the bottom of why I was so unhappy. Therapy helped me face the harsh reality that I disliked my work intensely, and that it held no positive meaning for me. In stepping back, I saw that I'd had burning fantasies for years about exciting new fields I wanted to be part of (the film industry, for one), but I hadn't taken any real steps toward transitioning to those fields. I'd been paralyzed by fear that I'd lose too much, or more precisely, that I'd lose what little power and self-esteem I'd derived from my money and title. I'd let my dreams die, chalking them up to childish longings that served no purpose. The worst blow yet was recognizing that I no longer liked or respected myself as a professional. I felt as if

I'd emerged from a twenty-year trance to the awareness that I'd always "done the right thing" for money, security, and safety, and this blind commitment to the right thing had stolen my life away.

The Breakdown Comes

After years of dissatisfaction and feeling inauthentic every day at work, the final straw-breaking blow came. Right after 9/11, I was laid off from my high-level position in a way that was brutal to my ego. It left me shattered and disillusioned. This devastation came only one month after moving to a larger house farther away from New York City, which meant more financial demands and less accessibility to other comparable jobs. My wake-up call had arrived.

Cast out from my job, I lost my corporate identity and self-worth. My sense of security was gone, and I felt depressed, disoriented, and alone. The experience felt like a sort of death, and with that "death" came denial, anger, bargaining, depression, and finally acceptance. As I later learned, these are the same stages of grief and loss identified by Elisabeth Kübler-Ross in her groundbreaking work on death and dying. This type of crisis affects the whole self—physical, emotional, mental, and spiritual. No single approach or technique is "the answer" when it comes to moving through breakdown to breakthrough.

A Breakthrough Emerges

Thanks to therapy, I chose to look at this crisis as a chance to turn my life around. I took a hard look at what led me into professional hell and became a student of life, relationships, work identity, and change. I jumped into earning a master's degree in marriage and family therapy, received coaching training, and became a psychotherapist and coach. I also studied hundreds of books, research studies, articles—anything I could get my hands on—about concepts of life change, professional crisis, transition, midlife staging, women's development, spirituality, health, family dynamics, communication and systems theory, theories of personality, and more.

Along the way, I was startled by the number of women I met who felt as overwhelmed and miserable as I had. I noticed, too, that while some people experience sudden and dramatic change as a crisis and suffer through it, some do not. I needed to understand why.

To learn more, I conducted a national research study on *Women Overcoming Professional Crisis: Finding New Meaning in Life and Work*, co-sponsored by the Esteemed Woman Foundation. Within the first thirty minutes of announcing my study via email, I received twenty responses from women across the country and outside the United States *asking* to participate. This work had hit a nerve! The research confirmed something quite amazing: in epidemic proportions, professional women are feeling disempowered and deeply dissatisfied in their professional lives, which in turn leads to other life crises. Ultimately, this dissatisfaction is about a breakdown in the relationships we forge and develop in four key areas: with ourselves, with others, with the world, and with our higher selves. New avenues for help must be found, and this book offers a solid start.

The Power of Stepping Back, Letting Go, and Saying Yes! to Yourself

Amid the thousands of women who are suffering from a lack of professional empowerment, many have taken courageous steps to face and let go of their limitations and fears, choosing a new path that leads to a life of passion, power, and purpose—in short, success and joy *on their terms*. *Breakdown, Breakthrough* presents their compelling and inspiring stories and offers accounts of professional women who have lived through the breakdown of feeling powerless and have overcome their challenges to reinvent themselves in creative, expansive, and meaningful ways from which we all can learn. They share their insights and lessons learned from stepping back to gain a new, widened perspective of their situation, shedding what holds them back and saying yes! to their power to make their life visions a reality.

What's Ahead

Breakdown, Breakthrough presents a coaching, behavioral, and spiritual framework for examining the patterns that contribute to the disempowerment women face today. This book explains how you can navigate successfully through these breakdown crises, or bypass them altogether, to achieve a more powerful, passionate, and purposeful life.

The introduction, "The Power of Yes!," explains what crisis and breakdown is, then describes the many benefits of walking away from disempowerment crises and saying yes! to yourself. You'll learn how these crises impact women, and you'll understand what it means to feel powerful in life and work.

Chapter 1, "Breakdown in Professional Women—Why Now?," explores the disempowerment phenomenon midlife professional women are facing. It presents key developmental issues and compelling data that reveal why professional women so often (and understandably) experience "breakdown" and wish to reevaluate their current path.

Chapter 2, "Recognizing When You're in Professional Crisis," will help you identify whether you are experiencing a disempowerment crisis or simply having "a tough time." It outlines the four areas of disempowerment that women typically face in midlife and helps you assess which are problematic for you.

In chapter 3, "A New Model for Empowered Living," we'll explore what full empowerment in life and work looks like. The chapter then provides a guide to understanding the root causes of the twelve disempowerment crises, along with the necessary shifts in thinking and action to overcome them. You'll learn about the power of stepping back, letting go, and saying yes! as key steps toward change.

Each of chapters 4 through 15 examines one of the twelve crises that constitute the full "I Can't Do This" phenomenon women are facing today. Chapter 4, "Resolving Chronic Health Problems," presents steps for understanding potential messages behind chronic illness as related to professional malaise.

In chapter 5, the crisis of "Overcoming Loss" reveals how losses in life often lead individuals to rethink their entire existence and focus on new life priorities that create a shift in their professional trajectory. Steps to help heal the emotions concerning loss, and to bring forward parts of yourself in the process, are offered.

Chapter 6, "Achieving Self-Love," examines ways women relinquish their authentic selves for success. It presents steps for understanding your authentic values, expressing your priorities, and reestablishing integrity and self-respect.

Chapter 7, "Speaking Up with Power," discusses how women are often unable to advocate for themselves, challenge the status quo, or speak up without fearing or experiencing punishment, criticism, or suppression. Approaches are given to help you understand ways that previous patterns and traumatic incidents of suppression in your life are still being reenacted.

Chapter 8, "Breaking Cycles of Mistreatment," provides tools for women to address abuse, diminishment, or disrespect. It offers steps to strengthen your boundaries, receive advocacy and support, and protect yourself from systems of mistreatment.

Have you awakened to the realization that continuing to compete, and doing what it takes to remain on top, is simply too difficult or no longer worthwhile? Chapter 9, "Shifting from Competition to Collaboration," presents steps for shedding the ego-based judgments and crushing competition that lead women to make the wrong choices for themselves. It offers approaches for taking a new life direction away from competition toward authentic values-based living.

Feeling completely stuck—in dissatisfying jobs, in restricting relationships—is a common phenomenon for women, and many see their paralysis as the result of financial constraints. Chapter 10, "Escaping Financial Traps," explains how to gain strength by revising negative beliefs and actions around money, power, and self-reliance.

Chapter 11, "Using Real Talents in Life and Work," looks at feeling powerless in your ability to use your gifts, talents, and abilities. It explains the importance of stepping up to use your talents and offers tools for helping you honor and express what you value.

Awakening to a sense of your own mortality and of a longing to make a difference in the world constitutes chapter 12's crisis, "Helping Others and the World." This chapter explores your longings for greater meaning and offers recommendations to propel you toward sustainable work that fulfills your life purpose.

Does everything feel like it's falling apart? Chapter 13, "Falling Together After Falling Apart," looks at the crisis of key areas in your life coming apart at the seams all at once. It explores steps for releasing your commitment to struggle, accepting positive possibilities, and creating your new life as you want it to be.

Chapter 14, "Balancing Life and Work," discusses the crisis of failing to balance the demands of work with other key life responsibilities. It uncovers habits of perfectionism and overfunctioning and discusses how to receive help to stop trying to achieve the impossible.

A large number of professional women have simply lost touch with who they are at the core. They struggle with the questions "Who am I in this world and what am I here to do?" Chapter 15, "Doing Work and Play That You Love," offers new approaches to saying yes! to knowing who you are and believing you can live a life of your dreams.

The concluding chapter, "Claiming Your Passion, Power, and Purpose," distills the most powerful advice interviewees have shared on ways to move through professional breakdown to breakthrough. This advice is straight from the hearts, minds, and souls of those who have overcome feeling powerless in life and work, and lived to tell the tale.

Real Stories/Real People

The stories presented here are real, based on interviews and conversations conducted in 2006–2007 with more than one hundred professional women across the country. Except where noted, the individuals' names are real. As far as possible, I've retained the specific details of each interviewee's inspiring story.

In some cases, at an interviewee's request, I've modified identifying information and events to maintain confidentiality. In others, to protect the privacy of the persons involved, I've merged specific details of two individuals' accounts.

Recommended Steps for Stepping Back, Letting Go, and Saying Yes!

There are thousands of ways to assist individuals who wish to change their lives. Many of these are effective, but no single approach works for everyone. The recommended exercises at the end of each chapter have been selected from years of training, study, and experience. The journal exercises help you *step back* for new perspective and gain a deeper connection to your inner thoughts and feelings. Use the *Breakdown, Breakthrough* Journal available at www.elliacommunications.com, or use your own. The coaching exercises offer approaches to *letting go* of limiting thoughts and actions, and *saying yes!* to what compels you.

These recommendations have one powerful trait in common: they draw on what you already know at your core. They honor you and how you view the world, and they foster self-acceptance while giving you the courage to move forward.

Here, you'll find women's courageous stories of breakdown to breakthrough, along with great advice for others.

What You May Expect Going Forward

Making lasting positive change is not easy, but the rewards are tremendous. As you go through this book and read about others' experience of breakdown to breakthrough, you may be surprised by new realizations. And unsettling emotions may surface. If this happens and you would like support, please see the helpful resources at the back of this book. Or you may wish to develop your own *Breakdown, Breakthrough* circle to explore this material and share your thoughts and progress on an ongoing basis.

In the end, *Breakdown, Breakthrough* will help you redefine success, purpose, and true quality of life in terms that are meaningful to you. Since I have personally experienced each and every one of these crises (some at the same time), I know that these crises can be not only survived but ultimately viewed as blessings that lead to an expansive and enriched life. Awakening to the realization that you are dissatisfied with your situation is the first step to changing it.

Use this book to start you on your way to breakthrough!

Breakdown, Breakthrough

INTRODUCTION

The Power of Yes!

* * *

Sweet are the uses of adversity.

WILLIAM SHAKESPEARE
As You Like It, Act 2, Scene 1

Defining Professional "Crisis"

What is true *crisis* in our lives? How can we tell we're heading into crisis, rather than simply going through a really bad time? What are the signs of breakdown? This chapter explains what professional crisis is for women today. You'll learn what working women lack when they are in crisis, as well as the many benefits of moving forward to breakthrough.

As defined in Webster's dictionary,[1] a "crisis" is:

- The turning point for better or worse, as in an acute disease or fever
- A paroxysmal attack of pain, distress, or disordered function
- An emotionally significant event or radical change of status in a person's life (a midlife *crisis*)
- The decisive moment (as in a literary plot)

- An unstable or crucial time or state of affairs in which a decisive change is impending; *especially* one with the distinct possibility of a highly undesirable outcome (a financial *crisis*)
- A situation that has reached a critical phase (the environmental *crisis*)

Clearly, we're talking about a no-turning-back situation—a time that calls for a reckoning and reevaluation. Crisis involves the occurrence of a deeply troubling, heart-wrenching, or grueling event or series of events that brings you to a recognition, finally and irrevocably, that change must occur *now*. Crisis pushes you to your knees and cracks open your awareness that to repeat this experience (feeling/event/situation) would be close to intolerable.

Breakdown in the professional arena means that you have discovered beyond a doubt that how you work, what you work on, who you work with, who you are when you work, or where you work—one or more of these elements are causing damage to you, your life, your body, and your spirit. Breakdown often seems to strike out of the blue, yet we rarely get to this point without warning signs along the way.

Crisis may look different for each person, but one unifying theme defines it: Crisis is a wake-up call that demands your attention and reveals that major change in life or work is required, and fast.

Why Focus on Professional Women in Crisis?

Women typically feel powerless and are breaking down in the professional arena in ways that men are not. This is not to say that men do not struggle with professional and personal crises; of course they do. In fact, many of the challenges discussed in this book will resonate with men. (Based on my many conversations with men, my next book may be *Breakdown, Breakthrough II* for men!)

Breakdown, Breakthrough is not about finding fault—in men or women. Thousands of women—myself included—can say that some of our best and strongest mentors have been men. Also, many women reveal that their most significant challenges have been with female bosses and colleagues. The goal of this book is not to focus on one specific professional dilemma, but to help you gain clarity on *your* personal and professional situation and identity—whatever it may be—to assist you in moving successfully through your challenges. To do so, we need a new model or guide for empowered living that speaks directly to each of our particular sets of challenges.

What Are Women in Crisis Lacking?

What are professional women longing for when breakdown occurs? Women who have gone through significant professional transition reveal that when they were in professional crisis, they struggled with the absence of one or more of the following benefits of a fully empowered life.

They yearned for, but couldn't find the way to:

- Honor or express their various facets
- Respect both the work they do and their colleagues, and be respected in turn
- Be treated fairly
- Earn the money they need to
- Expand their self-reliance
- Achieve "quality of life," flexibility, or control over what they do and how they do it
- Balance their numerous important life roles
- Make a significant positive difference in the world and in the lives of others
- Utilize their voices, talents, and abilities
- Contribute fully in ways that reflect their unique needs and values without being negatively judged or diminished

Professional breakdown, then, involves realizing that you are struggling—and failing—to attain a positive life experience that includes passion, power, purpose, security, integrity, self-reliance, and balance. For some, addressing crisis and making room for positive life change requires a good deal of inner and outer work. But for others, small tweaks in a critical dimension are enough.

For all individuals, breaking through to positive life change involves three powerful steps:

1. Step back to disentangle from your situation and gain a fresh, expanded perspective.
2. Let go of negative thinking and actions that hold you back.
3. Say yes! to honoring yourself and taking action toward what compels you.

Benefits of Addressing Crisis and Saying Yes! to Yourself

After living in the midst of crisis for a long time, women often feel chronically debilitated, depressed, angry, or sick. They may feel unable to live fully or experience meaning and joy, or be present for those they love and care for. Once you awaken to the sense that you are somehow thwarted and not living up to your potential, you feel discomfort and pain.

As you begin your exploration, the difficulty of your experiences may seem to be draining you of the energy needed to start the process of change. But those who have lived through this period have said, "Once I took the first step of examining what was not working, I began to feel hopeful that things could change. It seemed as if an enormous weight had lifted, and I knew then that I could do what I needed to."

The benefits of taking the first step, and gaining even small degrees of power to overcome professional breakdown, are enormous. You will begin to:

- Make friends with yourself and your body, and understand the information your physical condition reveals
- Enjoy stronger, healthier, more connected relationships that are based on empathy and respect rather than conflict and competition
- Recognize the influence of your ego and learn how to integrate it with other aspects of yourself
- Find enjoyable, purposeful work that sustains you
- Access inspiration and helpful support when you need it
- Discover your unique purpose that gives meaning to your life and work, and live from that knowledge each day
- Embrace change rather than fight it
- Live more joyfully and passionately
- Thrive and grow through life's challenges

The growth experience of breaking through your struggles transforms all aspects of your life. Ample evidence shows that women are finding new ways to successfully deal with major professional crises and are reaching new levels of success and satisfaction. Overcoming breakdown, and finding new meaning in life and work, is not only a possibility but a necessity—and a blessing—for thousands of women today.

THE DISEMPOWERMENT DILEMMA

1

Breakdown in Professional Women— Why Now?

*We shall not escape our dangers
by recoiling from them.*
WINSTON CHURCHILL

"Everything I've worked for *has just lost its importance to me. I really have no idea what to do or where to go next. I desperately want to do something different, something more meaningful to me, but I can't figure out what that is."*

"I feel so mistreated and unappreciated at work. What I really want to do is tell them all off, but I end up coming back each day, and stuffing down my anger and resentment."

"I can't keep up this pace. I want some time off, and I need more flexibility and space to be with my daughter. But how can I ask for that when I've just been promoted?"

"I feel sick and exhausted all the time, and I just can't beat this illness. I can barely function, at work or at home. I need a break!"

"If I really get honest with myself, I realize I'm just not performing at my peak anymore at this job. I'm not at my best anymore and it's scary to me."

"A friend of mine has her own small business, loves it, and makes great money without killing herself each day. I wish I could figure out how to do that, but I don't think I have what it takes to make it on my own."

I hear these and similar comments continually from professional women who have reached a critical turning point in their lives. After devoting years to building solid careers, they've discovered, sometimes in a flash and sometimes over the course of months or years, that their professional lives and identities simply no longer work. This experience—what I call a breakdown—is occurring with greater frequency and impact than ever before to professional women in the United States.

Professional Crises

Women today face many forms of professional crisis. Each revolves around powerlessness—perceived or real—to act positively and effectively on their own behalf. Whether it's being afraid to speak up; allowing themselves to be mistreated; doubting their capabilities or longings; resisting the truth; or acting in ways that are contrary to their values, disempowerment is at the heart of the problem.

When women feel powerless, they perceive themselves to be unable to affect positive change. They experience a persistent longing for acceptance and validation from others. They view themselves as small, ineffective, and unworthy—as hapless victims of circumstance incapable of charting their own course with a commanding hand or voice.

Empowered women, on the other hand, have conscious and direct access to their own vast capabilities, strengths, and gifts. They are aware of—and continually draw on—the deep wellspring of internal and external resources available to them, for their highest good and the good of others. They embrace change and transition, trusting themselves to weather any storm successfully. Somehow they believe that all will come out well in the end.

Why Crises for Working Women Now?

The current cultural and professional landscape for women reveals new trends affecting women's ability to succeed in the workplace and at home. While women have made great progress and are achieving new heights professionally, they are still fighting against some very tough odds.

According to Catalyst, a leading research and advisory organization devoted to expanding opportunities for women at work, recent changes in women's professional involvement and contribution in the United States have been dramatic.[1] Midlife women are experiencing newly forged independence, higher earning potential, and increased power and responsibility in the workplace. They are also experiencing greater access to higher education, which leads to increased professional prowess.[2] Nearly one-third of wives now outearn their husbands, and the proportion of women earning more than $100,000 has tripled in the past decade.[3]

Double Lives/Double Demands?

Women's professional contributions are on the rise, but a key question remains at the heart of their success in life and work: "What has shifted in women's lives to make way for this change?" Not enough, according to thousands.

While women have stepped up to carve out new and important professional identities, many remain constricted by outdated thinking and behavior. For instance, although women now make up nearly one-half of the U.S. labor force, the majority of domestic responsibility still falls to women, as does raising and caring for children and elderly family members. Dual-career families are on the rise, yet the availability of quality child care has not kept pace. Surprisingly, some people continue to believe that maternal employment is detrimental to children. Despite well-documented evidence that children can develop equally well regardless of the employment status of their parents, many working women are bitterly criticized for being both professionals and mothers.[4]

With the rise of mothers in the workforce comes the ever-important need for women to balance work with home life. The amount of leisure or free time has steadily decreased, and the associated stress in balancing full-time job demands with other responsibilities such as tending to a sick parent or spouse is escalating.[5] These added pressures create acute stress for women.

Not "Men in Skirts"

According to Sylvia Ann Hewlett's groundbreaking book, *Off-Ramps and On-Ramps,*[6] recent research has documented what you and I have known for years—women are not "men in skirts." Generally speaking, women have different professional values, motivations, needs, and desires than their male colleagues.

The following components are highly important to women in their work lives:

- Flexibility in their careers and schedules
- A healthy, satisfying balance between life and work
- Reasonable demands on their time in the office and in travel
- The ability to shift time and focus when important child- and elder-care needs emerge
- Respect for themselves, their work, their colleagues, and their supervisors
- A satisfying degree of control over their time, endeavors, and responsibilities
- The sense of contributing in a meaningful way to others and to society

Men, on the other hand, typically value power, recognition, responsibility, and compensation. When we look at the predominant setup of American corporations today, we see evidence of a white male competitive model. As Hewlett describes, this career model assumes a preference for linear, continuous employment history; an emphasis on full-time employment and "face" time; the expectation that an "ambitious" professional will exhibit the most intensive commitment in his or her 30s (or miss out forever on key opportunities for advancement); and, finally, that money is the primary motivator for professionals.

The assumptions of this model fly in the face of what many women need and want. One consequence of this ill-fitted model is that while women have the talent and ambition to perform outstandingly in the workplace, many are unwilling to fulfill these requirements over the long arch of their career. Why? Because these demands require too great a compromise in other life dimensions that women highly prize.

Midlife Crisis for Women Is Not a Myth

As those who are in midlife know all too well, the middle years of 35 to 55 represent a time of reckoning, reevaluation, and rethinking. One's perspective can shift radically. From the ages of 22 to 35, a committed professional spends an enormous amount of time, energy, and focus building her career to the level she desires. All of the accomplishments and accolades, however, come with personal sacrifices. These losses take on a very different meaning when viewed from the eyes of a 45-year-old.

Midlife individuals frequently awaken to brand new and startling realizations about what matters most. The glory of achievements and "winning at all costs" often fade. Other aspects of the human experience—helping, supporting, teaching, learning, growing, sharing, giving back, relishing life—become more compelling and meaningful. Dissatisfaction with who we are professionally becomes an urgent issue as we reach the middle years and look ahead to the future, glimpsing what might be waiting there.

At the same time, midlife women are going through dramatic personal change. As Sue Shellenbarger notes in *The Breaking Point*, there are currently 41.6 million baby-boomer women in the United States, and by age 50, more women than men are reporting a turbulent midlife transition. Based on recent studies, it has been forecasted that "more than 15 million U.S. women who are 38 to 55 years old will have, or are already having, what they regard as a midlife crisis—a staggering number about equal to the populations of Colorado, Massachusetts, and Minnesota combined."[7]

Midlife women are increasingly finding themselves in a host of new experiences that would have been inconceivable fifty years ago. Divorce rates for midlife women are on the rise, and women are initiating these divorces more often than men.[8] New life situations include blended families, single parenting, and dating. While life-changing events often lead women to reinvent themselves, adjusting and reconstructing requires tremendous effort and energy.

What's It All Mean?

Many factors are colliding at this time, bringing about a radical shift in what women want to achieve. Women now hold completely different expectations and longings than those of previous generations. This shift brings with it new beliefs about what is important in life, and what women are capable of. Role models from previous generations don't offer guidance on how to achieve a healthy, balanced, and meaningful professional and personal life. Today's midlife women may have grown up believing they could "have it all," but now that they have it, they're not sure it's worth keeping.

The critical thing to realize is that if you are a professional woman longing for a radical change in how you work and live, you are not alone. There are many solid, reasonable, well-founded, and well-documented reasons for what you're experiencing. Simply put, thousands of women in this country view life as unsatisfying, challenging, and exhausting—for many, it's a struggle. But we can't help ourselves if we continue to hide how we feel.

Let's face it: we all can't be wrong!

Can Women Achieve Breakthrough and Find Passion, Power, and Purpose?

The answer is a resounding "YES!" But not without significantly revising our individual and collective thinking, assumptions, and behavior. When women experience crisis, they often think, "How did I blow this?" and "When will I be found out?"

What I'm proposing here is a revision to that line of thinking. I'm suggesting that you stop in your tracks when facing crisis and begin to ask different questions than you're used to, questions that allow the possibility that this situation is occurring for a critical reason you are meant to address, for the betterment of yourself and others, challenging as it may be to do so.

Asking yourself "What am I meant to learn from this, and what changes am I needing to make in my life?" is a powerful start to examining the process of living, rather than just the content of your life.

2

Recognizing When You're in Professional Crisis

* * *

You gain strength, courage, and confidence
by every experience in which you really
stop to look fear in the face. You must do the
thing which you think you cannot do.

ELEANOR ROOSEVELT
You Learn by Living, 1960

THE DISEMPOWERMENT DILEMMA

In my work with clients, I have been amazed at women's depth of denial when things are bad. Women have said to me as we begin our work together that the term "crisis" doesn't fit their experience, or they feel "uncomfortable" using the word. Then they go on to describe deep pain, fear, a sense of isolation, hopelessness, and a host of other agonizing emotions. Women might say, "I'm just going through a bad patch" or "I'm having a hard time right now," but when they feel safe, they begin to expose the depth of their unhappiness. This acknowledgment paves the way for a probing new line of self-questioning to emerge. They begin to ask themselves, "You mean I may not have to live like this forever?" This chapter will help you determine if you are in fact experiencing a true professional crisis or simply going through "a tough time." You'll learn about the four levels of disempowerment women typically experience and identify which, if any, are problematic for you.

I've wondered why women habitually deny the existence of their anguish. Why are women so reluctant to call a spade a spade? I believe this denial of pain goes back to our socialization as children (perhaps it involves a bit of what we've picked up on our evolutionary journey as well). Research has shown that even as early as the teen years, girls begin to go underground with their emotions and start what seems to be a lifelong tendency of "stuffing down" their true feelings. Young women do not wish to appear weak or vulnerable; they are afraid of not measuring up to a stronger, more competent ideal; or they want to avoid being scrutinized or criticized.[1] Even more insidious is the "good girl" syndrome, which demands that they avoid actions that might rock the boat, challenge authority, or make others unhappy with them.

Many baby-boomer women were raised by well-meaning parents whose generation believed it was unladylike or worse for women to stand up for themselves. We are still battling the unstated injunction that we must be polite, "grin and bear it," lest we come across as whiners, nags, or the kind of women who are "just never satisfied."

To change this situation, women have to get real—with themselves and others—about their true feelings and thoughts about how their lives are going. If you feel an urgent need to alter your life, then it's time to do it.

How Can You Tell If You're in Breakdown and Need Change?

Women today face a myriad of challenges in both professional and personal arenas that share one theme—feeling powerless. "Disempowerment" here refers to the significant, persistent gap in an individual's ability to mold her life to her own satisfaction and fulfillment. This experience is widespread among women. I call it the "I Can't Do This" phenomenon, because thousands believe they simply can't do it—they can't direct their lives as they wish. They feel overwhelmed with what's on their plate, yet limited in their ability to bring about the changes they long for. This perceived powerlessness is damaging. It generates depression, anger, confusion, and paralysis, and it exacerbates other problems. In short, it causes "breakdown." "Breakdown" is a heart-wrenching, deeply disturbing, or shocking event or series of events that makes you understand, irrevocably, that change must occur *now*. If you are desperately longing for change, then crisis is most likely at hand. If you are chronically unhappy, resentful, or depleted—in short, *miserable*—then breakdown is at your door. Breakdown in the professional arena means that a key aspect of your professional identity and endeavors, or your way of integrating your professional life with your personal life, is no longer acceptable to you. Breakdown slaps you across the face and yells from inside you, *"So, what are you going to do now, huh? You know this can't continue!"*

Crisis is not a "bad" thing. It's not something to be ashamed of. It doesn't mean you're a failure. Yes, it's deeply painful—and you don't want to face it. But breakdown represents a critical turning point that can, if you let it, lead to something much better. Breakdown is a call for change, and for many people, radical change is the only door that opens to happiness, growth, and strength. I've lived through all twelve disempowerment crises myself, and I now consider them to be precisely what paved the way for my life to become what it is—meaningful, joyful, and satisfying.

Four Levels of Disempowerment

The text below describes the four levels of disempowerment that professional women experience, along with the three specific crises that characterize each level. The list begins with the most fundamental relational level and proceeds to the more far-reaching dimensions outside of yourself. This chapter will help you understand what disempowerment looks and feels like, and it will guide you in exploring the areas in which you may feel powerless in life and work.

Disempowerment in Relationship with Self

When you are disempowered at this level, you are limited in the degree to which you accept and value yourself. You suffer from feeling unworthy, small, and inferior. You jump through hoops in order to win your own validation and approval. But despite your Herculean efforts, you typically fail. Being stuck at this level indicates the need to focus on new thinking and actions that facilitate a reconnection to your inner being, to the worthiness of who you are at your core, and to the universal life force flow and the guidance it offers.

The three crises on this level are:

1. "I Can't Resolve My Health Problems." This is a crisis of failing health or a chronic physical ailment that has not been addressed effectively. You know you are facing this crisis when chronic illness emerges suddenly and won't respond to treatment. You sense that something larger is involved, something that impedes your ability to express and honor yourself, get rid of what's no longer needed, see and hear clearly what is going on around you, or protect yourself.

2. "I Can't Get Over This Loss." When you lose a colleague, friend, spouse, or loved one suddenly (whether the loss is due to death or other circumstances), your world can be turned upside down. Realizing you've lost an aspect of yourself or your self-identity can feel like a death. Deep loss can cause you to dramatically reevaluate where you are headed. You know you are facing this crisis when you can't seem to move forward after losing something or someone you love.

3. "I Can't Stand Who I've Become." In this crisis, your values, conduct, integrity, and behavior have been compromised for financial security, ego gratification, or mere survival in a hellish work environment. You know you are facing this crisis when you recognize that your thinking and behavior have become negative and destructive. You are not the person you were in the past, nor the person you want to be.

Disempowerment in Relationship with Others

When disempowered at this level, you have great difficulty speaking up for yourself effectively, without fear of repercussions. Your relationships are unsatisfying, and you find yourself in competitive and hostile interactions. You continually feel unworthy and afraid of being "found out," as if you're an impostor. Overall, you feel ill-treated and not respected. Experiencing challenge at this level points to the need to step up to your innate power. Moving forward becomes possible when you let go of your critical judgments and develop stronger boundaries that protect and support you.

The three crises on this level are:

4. "I Can't Speak Up Without Being Punished." This is a crisis of not being able to advocate effectively for yourself. You know you are facing this crisis when every time you speak up about something challenging, you fear facing punishment, criticism, or rejection.

5. "I Can't Stop the Abuse or Mistreatment I'm Experiencing." Being treated poorly by your employer or colleagues affects all aspects of your life. You know you are facing this crisis when your company and colleagues treat you intolerably, yet you remain in your job.

6. "I Can't Keep Up with This Competition." This crisis involves the disturbing realization that doing what it takes to compete and remain on top now feels too difficult or pointless. You know you are facing this crisis when the cut-throat mentality at work is taking a serious toll on you and is bleeding into other areas of your life.

Disempowerment in Relationship with the World

Feeling powerless in your relationship with the world means you feel chewed up and spit out. The world doesn't seem friendly or forgiving. You can't find effective ways to navigate through your challenges, or to utilize your talents and gifts in ways that feel joyful and satisfying. You struggle with power and money (most often from their lack) and feel incapable of charting your own course with confidence and optimism. Experiencing crisis at this level reflects a need to explore essential truths about yourself and your life.

The three crises on this level are:

7. "I Can't Get Out of This Financial Trap." In this crisis, you believe you must remain in an unfulfilling or intolerable job, relationship, or situation because of money constraints. You know you are facing this crisis when you've given up everything that matters to you, for money.

8. "I Can't Use My Real Talents in Life and Work." This crisis occurs when you realize that you are not using your natural talents and gifts, but you desperately long to. You know you are facing this crisis when your work no longer fits, and you fantasize regularly about moving to a different job or field but take no action.

9. "I Can't Help Others and the World." A very common professional crisis involves awakening to your own mortality, and to a deep longing to make a difference in the world but not knowing how. You know you are facing this crisis when you have an urgent longing to do more positive work.

Disempowerment in Relationship with Higher Self

Disempowerment at this level signifies your longing to connect with the more expansive aspects of yourself and your spirit. You wish to receive more help in your life and work, but you can't stop overfunctioning and overcontrolling. Crisis at this level is a wake-up call to remind you that you are an indispensable part of life, that you have deep value and significance. But this significance can be realized only when you tap into the power, intuition, and guidance of your higher self.

The three crises on this level are:

10. "I Can't Hold Things Together Any Longer." The crisis of "falling apart"—when everything all at once comes apart at the seams—brings you to your knees. This crisis causes you to reprioritize your focus and energy on what matters most. You know you are facing this crisis when dealing with everything in your life is impossible.

11. "I Can't Balance My Life and Work." This crisis is one of attempting, but failing, to balance the demands of your work life with the requirements of your other roles and responsibilities. You know you are facing this crisis when you're exhausted and at wit's end, and you feel like you're failing at what matters most to you.

12. "I Can't Find or Do Work and Play That I Love." Many professional women have simply lost touch with who they are. They struggle with "Who am I in this world? What do I want to be known for? What am I here to do? What do I love to do, and how can I incorporate that into a fulfilling career?" This crisis points to your need to reconnect with the *real* you. You know you are facing this crisis when you feel your life doesn't match you. Although you desperately want out of your current line of work or situation, you believe it's impossible for several "good" reasons.

MOVING FORWARD TO BREAKTHROUGH

Say YES to yourself today, and take this assessment below. By answering these questions as honestly and critically as you can, you will 1) understand if you are in crisis, and 2) learn which of the four levels of disempowerment is most relevant to your situation.

The First Step: Assessing If You Are in Crisis

The first step is to evaluate your situation as clearly and honestly as possible, with your own set of standards and measures. It's time to forge a deeper, more loving and accepting relationship with yourself. Consider your own thoughts and experiences as the highest authority. Forget what your friends, colleagues, husband, parents, and children say you should feel, do, and believe.

Take this assessment as many times as possible throughout your reading of this book (and beyond), and see how your answers change over time.

There are no right or wrong answers here. This assessment is your chance to get to know yourself better, to be completely honest and open. Leave your perfectionism and ego at the door. Now is the time to get "hip to your trip."

Find a quiet, comfortable, and private place, with a comfy pillow to lean on. Turn off the cell phone and turn down the answering machine, close the door, and focus just on *you*.

1. Ponder and answer these questions as deeply and honestly as you can in your journal:

    a. Are you *fulfilled and satisfied* with your life choices?   Yes   No

    b. Do you *feel good* about yourself, your life, and where you are going?   Yes   No

    c. Do you *trust you have what it takes* to continually create a satisfying life of passion, power, and purpose?   Yes   No

Question 1 Assessment

If you answered "Yes" to all of these questions, then you are moving in a positive and satisfying direction. If you answered "No" to any of them, your life is asking you to step up to change, and this book will help.

2. On a scale of 1 to 10 (1 means "Very Far Away" and 10 means "Very Close"), answer the following questions. *Circle the number that best represents your life today.* To help you avoid "5"—which leaves you on the fence—"X" appears in its place. Push yourself in one direction or another.

    a. How close are you to being as powerful and self-assured as you'd like to be in life and work?

        Very Far Away   Very Close

            1   2   3   4   X   6   7   8   9   10

    b. How close are you to living a life that gives you passion and joy?

        Very Far Away   Very Close

            1   2   3   4   X   6   7   8   9   10

    c. How close are you to living a life of purpose and meaning?

        Very Far Away   Very Close

            1   2   3   4   X   6   7   8   9   10

What would you need to do differently to answer these questions with a "10"?

Question 2 Assessment

If you answered "4" or lower to any of the above questions, you may be struggling with how to integrate what you feel you *have to do* in life to be successful with how you *want to live* your life. You are wishing for a deeper sense of purpose, joy, and integrity.

3. Review the list of statements below, and honestly ask yourself, "Does this reflect what I'm going through today?" *Check all that apply.*

    a. ( ) Successfully balancing my home life and work life feels almost impossible right now.

    b. ( ) I'm having chronic health problems that aren't getting better.

    c. ( ) I've lost someone or something I deeply loved, and I feel changed because of it.

d. (   ) I feel like things are falling apart in my life.

e. (   ) I've been treated poorly at work, and I don't feel the same about being there as I used to.

f. (   ) It seems like every time I speak up, I get squashed or punished.

g. (   ) I have gifts and talents that I'm not using, but I deeply long to.

h. (   ) In some ways, I don't like or respect who I've become.

i. (   ) I dislike what I do and am bored by it, but I have no idea what other work I could do.

j. (   ) My financial situation is keeping me trapped at work (or at home).

k. (   ) I just don't want to keep competing. I'm worn out.

l. (   ) I want to help people somehow, in a bigger way than I'm doing, but I don't know how.

Question 3 Assessment

If you checked any of the above statements, *it's time to make a change.* Transition is occurring, which can be very positive, if you are willing to embrace it and understand what the underlying issues suggest.

If You Checked Off	*Your Potential Crisis*	*Your Empowerment · Challenge Is With*
A	Balancing life and work	Higher self
B	Chronic health issues	Self
C	Suffering from loss	Self
D	Life is falling apart	Higher self
E	Cycles of mistreatment	Others
F	Speaking up with power	Others
G	Using talents in life and work	World
H	Self-loathing	Self
I	Can't find work I love	Higher self
J	Financial trap	World
K	Crushing competition	Others
L	Helping others	World

✳ STEP BACK

Write in your journal about what you learned from taking this assessment:

- Which empowerment level needs your attention most right now: Relationship with Self, Others, World, or Higher Self?
- What particular crisis within that level seems to be causing you the most difficulty?

✳ LET GO

What can you *let go of* in your life to free up energy and time to focus on what's important to you?

✳ SAY YES!

Choose one area to focus on this month, to gain empowerment as you go forward. Use this book as your tool for breakthrough.

The key area I will focus on to gain empowerment is: _____

Great job! You did it. Completing this assessment is the first and most important step you can take on the path to breaking through crisis to gain empowerment. You must know what isn't working in your life to determine where to begin changing it. Congratulations for having the courage to start.

3

A New Model for Empowered Living

* * *

*Courage is not the absence of despair;
it is, rather, the capacity to
move ahead in spite of despair.*

ROLLO MAY

THE DISEMPOWERMENT DILEMMA

Building on Abraham Maslow's model of the hierarchy of needs,[1] I conceive of empowerment in life and work as a four-level continuum. Empowerment begins with the most basic human relationship—your relationship with yourself. If your self-concept and way of viewing yourself is secure and loving, you have the foundation for constructing positive, healthy relationships with others. As this is achieved, you gain strength and support to become effective in the world, using your abilities for your own good and for the good of the world around you. Finally, empowerment builds to the most expansive dimension—your relationship with your higher self. Empowerment at this level allows you to tap into a breadth of abilities, perspective, and knowledge that is otherwise not available.

Beginning with a look at full empowerment, this chapter demystifies the twelve common crises women face today by revealing what is missing or what needs to be revised for empowerment to grow. It identifies the potential root of each crisis and offers specific recommendations for shifts in thinking and behavior that will help you gain strength in the areas where you most need it. By the end of this chapter, you'll know which crisis is most relevant to you at this time. You'll also understand what is necessary to resolve it, in order to claim passion, power, and purpose in your life and work.

Full Empowerment in Life and Work

Full empowerment in life and work means that you can say the following:

- I feel great about myself.
- I relate well, lovingly, and respectfully with others.

- I use my talents and gifts joyfully to make a difference.
- I meet my financial needs successfully.
- I have balance and harmony in my life and work.
- I live and behave authentically, in alignment with who I am inside.
- I am connected to higher-level support, wisdom, and guidance.
- I am powerful, and I can create the life I desire.

If the statements above reflect how you feel about yourself and your life today, congratulations! You are empowered. You can successfully handle all types of challenges that come your way, and you are able to shape your life as you dream it to be. If, however, you are less than fully empowered in one or more of these areas, it simply means that there is room for you to grow. To understand where to begin your empowerment development, let's explore what full empowerment means on each relational level: with self, others, the world, and the higher self.

I. Relationship with Self

At the root level of empowerment in life and work is your relationship with yourself. This involves the way in which you connect with and experience your core being, and the degree to which you honor and esteem your natural self. The more empowered you are at this level, the more unconditional your regard for yourself. You are not constantly seeking outside acceptance, validation, and love from others. When empowered, you love and honor your physical being. You understand that your body facilitates what you are here to achieve. You are conscious of, and view with kindness and acceptance, all key aspects of your nature.

II. Relationship with Others

This level represents how you communicate and interact with others. It involves how you perceive yourself in relation to other people. When empowered at this level, you are an effective communicator and an empathic listener, and you nurture yourself and others. You are as comfortable advocating for yourself as you are for others, and you use your voice in loving but commanding, compelling ways. You understand that we're all interconnected. You value interdependence and acknowledge the dynamics of circularity (I impact you/you impact me). You are drawn to pursuits that both bolster you and support others. At this level of empowerment, "winning at all costs" and deliberately climbing over others to achieve superiority is not only unappetizing but undesirable.

III. Relationship with the World

This level involves your ability to be an effective, positive instrument in service to the larger world. When you are empowered at this level, you view yourself as important, valuable, and useful to others. You've found meaning and purpose in your life. You feel energized by who you are and what you're doing, and you are excited about living in today's world, despite the many complex challenges you face.

IV. Relationship with Higher Self

When empowered at this final level, you gain access to the vast wisdom, resources, and knowledge of the collective mind, above and beyond your individual capabilities. You feel deeply connected—to yourself, to others, to your world, and to a higher source of creative power that lives within each of us. You honor the divine that is within you and within everyone else. You accept and embrace others' differences, and you focus on what is positive, exciting, and enriching in your life, not on what is negative and irritating. You say YES! to all aspects of a joyful, fulfilled life and feel worthy of it. You're aware of the tremendous creative power you have to make a difference in the world, and you're excited about stepping into this power. You know that you have support, and that a broader perspective is available whenever you ask for it. You know, too, that whatever occurs in life brings with it a potential for growth and expansion. You embrace challenge and change as a way to grow and be all that you can be.

A representation of the Hierarchy of Empowerment Needs in life and work appears on page 26. This hierarchy is depicted as a pyramid that consists of four levels regarding one's relationship with self, others, the world, and the higher self.

The lowest level is associated with needs for nurturing the self, including accepting, loving, and honoring yourself, and being able to openly express the basic dimensions of your personality. In the middle levels, needs pertaining to relating effectively with others and applying yourself in positive ways in the world are addressed. The top level pertains to needs associated with expansion, life balance, inspiration, and authentic living. At the top level you experience the deepest connection to your inner self, your

Honoring your values,
achieving balance, and
accessing inspiration
for authentic living

Fulfilling your financial needs,
using your talents in life and work,
and making a difference

Advocating for yourself, being treated with love
and respect, and feeling worthy of others' love

Honoring your physical self, expressing all aspects
of your basic nature, and achieving self-love

HIGHER SELF

WORLD

OTHERS

SELF

HIERARCHY OF EMPOWERMENT NEEDS

creative power, and higher dimensions of living and being. These top-level needs revolve around forming and maintaining a close relationship with higher-source wisdom, support, and guidance.

Self needs must be met first. Once these are met, we seek to satisfy needs about relating to others and having an impact on the world. The highest needs are about being all you can be in this lifetime, and doing so joyfully, feeling supported and connected to all that is. The higher needs in this hierarchy come into focus only when the lower needs are satisfied. Once an individual has moved up to the next level, needs in the lower level are no longer a priority. If a lower set of needs is no longer being met, you will temporarily reprioritize by focusing attention on the unfulfilled needs, but you will not permanently regress to the lower level. For instance, a high-level professional woman who experiences a serious illness may spend time focused on her physical needs (Self), but she will continue to attend to the needs of her family (Others) and her professional endeavors (World) and will likely return to focusing on her professional activities and goals after the illness has been addressed.

A Guide to Gaining Empowerment

Living in full empowerment is possible, as many can attest. But thousands of us struggle with challenges that keep us from a full and powerful connection with ourselves, our lives, our world, and our higher selves.

It has been said that no problem can be solved at the same level of consciousness that created it. I believe that causes underlie each disempowerment crisis. But only after you step back to gain an expanded perspective of the contributing factors can new possibilities emerge. Doing the inner and outer work to explore and address your challenges brings more positive shifts in your thinking and behavior. In this way, empowerment grows.

Pages 28–35 provide a synthesized guide to the essential steps for overcoming each crisis of disempowerment. These steps involve STEPPING BACK to gain perspective, LETTING GO of actions and beliefs that keep you stuck, and SAYING YES! to yourself and to new self-affirming actions and thoughts. Let go of pessimistic and negative actions and beliefs, which are often remnants from others' experiences. Say yes! to beliefs and behaviors that are positive and proactive, reflective of the human spirit's creative and expansive nature.

EMPOWERMENT GUIDE

I. EMPOWERMENT WITH SELF

EMPOWERMENT CRISIS	STEP BACK TO EXPLORE	LET GO
Resolving Chronic Health Problems	The body is communicating what the lips are not.	LET GO of ignoring or resisting *what is*.
Overcoming Loss	Grieving lost parts of yourself.	LET GO of overidentifying with one aspect.
Achieving Self-Love	Needing to reclaim your power from a source outside of you.	LET GO of giving up your power to others or things.

SAY YES!	BREAKTHROUGH	BEST ADVICE
SAY YES! to hearing your body, your intuition, and your heart.	"I am healthy and strong."	· Hear your body. · Heed your intuition. · Follow your heart.
SAY YES! to healing lost parts of yourself.	"I am integrated and whole."	· Bring suppressed parts forward. · Avoid overidentification. · Find a "better way."
SAY YES! to acting in alignment with the *real* you.	"I love and accept myself."	· Discover where you are being false. · Find the power inside you. · Disentangle from your struggle.

II. EMPOWERMENT WITH OTHERS

EMPOWERMENT CRISIS	STEP BACK TO EXPLORE	LET GO
Speaking Up with Power	Reliving past trauma over speaking up.	LET GO of your pain from past suppression.
Breaking Cycles of Mistreatment	Boundaries in need of strengthening.	LET GO of your belief in your powerlessness.
Shifting from Competition to Collaboration	Feeling the need to prove your worth over and over.	LET GO of feeling "not good enough."

SAY YES!	BREAKTHROUGH	BEST ADVICE
SAY YES! to your personal power through words and action.	"I use my voice to support myself and others."	· Say what you want to say. · Use positive language. · Heal past suppression.
SAY YES! to developing healthy boundaries.	"I am treated with love and respect."	· Develop healthy boundaries. · Stop pleasing others to fill your needs. · Get advocacy.
SAY YES! to your innate worthiness and value.	"I am enough."	· Heal not feeling good enough. · Look at the cost of "winning at all costs." · Get real—you don't want to play this game.

III. EMPOWERMENT WITH THE WORLD

EMPOWERMENT CRISIS	STEP BACK TO EXPLORE	LET GO
Escaping Financial Traps	Valuing money above all else.	LET GO of beliefs, relationships, and actions that keep you small.
Using Real Talents in Life and Work	Denying the power of your unique gifts.	LET GO of your fears of failure and inadequacy.
Helping Others and the World	Resisting the fact that you can make a difference.	LET GO of believing you don't have what it takes.

SAY YES!	BREAKTHROUGH	BEST ADVICE
SAY YES! to a balanced relationship with money.	"I fulfill my financial needs and honor who I am."	· Balance your money relationship. · Know what you long to do and honor it. · Shed what keeps you down.
SAY YES! to believing in your talents without fail.	"I use my real talents in life and work."	· Know your natural talents. · Get solid in your belief in yourself. · Be open to angels in your life.
SAY YES! to changing the world.	"I help others and the world."	· Stop resisting your new path. · Enjoy life's preciousness. · Trust you can help the world.

IV. EMPOWERMENT WITH HIGHER SELF

EMPOWERMENT CRISIS	STEP BACK TO EXPLORE	LET GO
Falling Together After Falling Apart	A connection to struggle and to what no longer serves.	LET GO of making excuses.
Balancing Life and Work	Overfunctioning and perfectionism to control your world.	LET GO of your fears about not being in control.
Doing Work and Play You Love	Believing others who say you should let your dreams go.	LET GO of "shoulding."

SAY YES!	BREAKTHROUGH	BEST ADVICE
SAY YES! to creating your new life as you want it.	"I know what is important to me, and I honor it."	· Stop making excuses. · Get someone to hold you accountable. · Find a powerful role model.
SAY YES! to being helped by others and your higher self.	"I balance my life and work with joy."	· Stop overfunctioning. · Address what you fear most. · Get help from others and your higher self.
SAY YES! to doing what you can't live without.	"My work and play represent the real *Me*."	· Relax, it's not all up to you. · Reconcile making a living doing what you must. · Get higher source help.

Fundamentals of Empowerment Work

To overcome feeling powerless and to ensure that negative situations will not be repeated, you need to gain awareness of where you lack ability to move forward. Taking positive action—unlike any you've tried before—will reverse habitual negative patterns and help you trust your own internal strength, value, and capabilities.

As you make progress, new doors will open to you and options will expand. In doing this work, you will notice shifts in your experiences and in what emerges. You will have more hope and understanding, and you will know that what appears in your life can be used as tools for your growth.

Those who have achieved true empowerment in life and work can say, *"What I do for my work and play represents the real me. I value and cherish myself and others, and I have found peace, joy, fulfillment, love, and meaning in my life."*

A Loving Relationship with Self Is Key

A loving, accepting relationship with yourself is essential to achieve empowerment at other levels. If you are experiencing gaps in your self-acceptance and self-esteem, or if physical ailments or emotional disturbances have not been responsive to healing, these problems need to be addressed first. Once you have developed a kinder, more loving relationship with yourself, moving to the next level of empowerment is possible.

Growth Occurs in a Nonlinear Way

At different times, you may move up or down a level of empowerment, depending upon particular life circumstances. An outside crisis such as serious illness or the death of a loved one may present new challenges that send you back a level to help you deal with unresolved issues.

Expansion and Growth Are Continual

Each level of empowerment represents new challenges and opportunities, but you're never "done." Once you reach the level of empowerment with higher self, different challenges will allow you to achieve an even broader perspective. Each crisis points to a need to access your inner power, honor yourself more fully to make use of this power, and focus your power for your good and that of others. Once you've unlocked the underlying meaning of each crisis, these situations will cease to rock you to your core—you will have developed the necessary tools to address your challenges more quickly and easily.

Facing Multiple Crises Is Not Unusual

Experiencing different crises at several levels at the same time is not uncommon. When this occurs, focus your efforts on your relationship with yourself, then on your relationship with others. These efforts will give you strength and support to address the farther-reaching challenges.

What's Ahead

In the coming chapters, you will hear compelling and inspiring stories of real women who have navigated through the twelve disempowerment crises and been transformed. Each woman, through her journey, gained much-needed perspective and took new, proactive steps to move successfully through her challenges to a new level of living.

The chapters also provide commentary on what each woman learned and how she achieved the passion, power, and purpose she so longed for. These women share their fabulous advice and explain how reinventing aspects of themselves was not only called for, but a blessing that changed their lives.

MOVING FORWARD TO BREAKTHROUGH

The exercises in the *Moving Forward to Breakthrough* section in this chapter and all subsequent chapters aim to connect you more deeply to yourself, and to help you *Step Back* to explore your situation from a new vantage point. You will also be given exercises to *Let Go* of what isn't working and *Say Yes!* to new positive and powerful thoughts, beliefs, and actions. These will fuel your strength and confidence and help you direct your life in satisfying, enriching ways.

✳ STEP BACK

Review the Empowerment Guide (pp. 28–35).

- Which crisis resonates most deeply with you now?
- How do you *know* you're not where you want to be in this area?
- What are your thoughts when you read the "Breakthrough" listed for that crisis? Can you say that statement today? Is it something you'd like to be able to say?

✳ LET GO

Forgiveness is essential to letting go of pent-up resentment, pain, and disappointment. When you release your anger and your feelings of being wronged, you make room for more positive feelings, experiences, and events.

- Who are you harboring a deep resentment against?
- What do you need to do to let go of this burden and forgive this individual, once and for all, and be done with it?
- Can you do this today? If not, when and how? Forgiving is a choice, and this choice is up to you.
- After you forgive this individual, write in your journal about what comes into your life because of the fresh, clean space you created.

✳ SAY YES!

Review the Empowerment Guide about the possible underlying issues of the crisis (or crises) you selected. In your journal, record your thoughts on the following questions.

- How does this underlying issue apply to you?
- How does the *Let Go* and *Say Yes!* information relate to you and your life at this time?
- With regard to this empowerment challenge you face today, what do you think *specifically* needs to be modified in your life for you to be happier and more satisfied?
- Brainstorm new ways that you might gain additional support in exploring where your life is not working as well you wish.

EMPOWERMENT WITH SELF

4

Resolving Chronic
Health Problems

A bodily disease which we look upon
as whole and entire within itself,
may, after all, be but a symptom
of some ailment in the spiritual part.

NATHANIEL HAWTHORNE

EMPOWERMENT WITH SELF

* **STEP BACK TO EXPLORE** The body is communicating what the lips are not.

* **LET GO** of ignoring or resisting *what is*.

* **SAY YES!** to hearing your body, your intuition, and your heart.

* **BREAKTHROUGH**
"I am healthy and strong."

* **Helen:** *Here I was, a top administrator in a large city public library system, and the stress of it was killing me. I was working a zillion hours, and it was all administrative—I wasn't working with children or books, both of which I loved. I knew I had to leave, but it's really hard to leave a job that you create. Anyway, I did it, I left, but then I needed another job quick. So I took a position that focused on teaching librarians how to use the Internet. I worked on computers all day, every day, and let me tell you, computers aren't my thing. It was all-encompassing, and I hated the computer aspect. I then began to have these terrible dizzy spells—blinding spells that made me nauseous and weak, and I couldn't see. It was so painful to use my eyes in any way, to read the computer screen, to read books. I felt dizzy and sick all the time. Imagine a librarian not being able to read books, books that I had so loved. I went to doctor after doctor, and nobody could get to the bottom of it. I grew allergic to my contacts, and I couldn't wear my glasses either. Nothing was working. I had so much stress, just dealing with feeling sick all the time and trying to hold it together for my little children. On top of that, I was dealing with my mother's decline into dementia with Alzheimer's, and the sudden death of my cousin from cancer. It just was all too much. But I always had a gut feeling that my dizziness was about being on the wrong path, doing the wrong work.*

Helen is describing her debilitating eye disorder that, despite her long and hard efforts to find effective treatment or a cure, would not be alleviated until she relieved the stress she was bearing from her job. This experience is all too common among professional women—suffering from physical ailments that recur and break the body down over time. Traditional medical approaches often are limited in their capability to successfully treat these illnesses. Only when individuals remove the stress, helpless-

---

* Helen is a 48-year-old former director of a grant project in the Chicago Public Library system.   41

ness, and frustration of their current paths do they find themselves on the road back to health.

Clearly, a very strong mind-body-spirit connection exists. Many people resist this concept, but to me such resistance is a denial of what is simply right in front of us—a far more expansive view of what our human physicality means and represents. My wake-up call on this front occurred when I experienced severe and recurring tracheitis that would not be cured. For four years I was plagued with recurrent pain, loss of voice, throat infection, fever, and exhaustion. Doctors couldn't figure out why I kept having these troubles and just gave me antibiotics, which created more health problems. So, at my wit's end, I consulted an energy healer a friend had recommended.

This energy healer said, "Kathy, this pain and illness in your throat is like a 'crying within,' a sign that you are not being true to yourself, or speaking truth for yourself. What kind of work do you do?" As I described my work and how miserable I was, the healer continued, "You see, this work, this job, doesn't reflect the real you at all—it's a farce, a sham for you. Your illness is a message, communicated over and over, that you are using the seat of your expression—your voice—in ways that are contrary to who you really are. You need to find a way to be more true to yourself, to express yourself honestly and openly. What's going on at work? Are you being mistreated? Are they doing things you don't agree with there?" Of course, the answer was YES! on all fronts. She concluded, "I think you need a new job or profession, and you shouldn't wait."

The healer saw what I couldn't—the professional road I'd taken for years was a false and demeaning one. But I was too "stuck" to face it. I couldn't speak up for myself. Nor was I speaking up to myself about how much I disliked my work and the lack of meaning in it. Illness brought me to the realization that I couldn't wait any longer to make a change—now was the time.

How do we overcome chronic illness? One potent way is to understand what your illness is saying to you. For me, I realized that my throat problem was telling me to speak up for myself. So I began to. I decided to tell the truth as best I could, whenever I could, and be honest with myself and others. I admitted out loud when things weren't working. This one act was extremely challenging for me, but I knew it was essential to live a happy, healthy life. I promised too that I would never go back to doing work merely to make money, a soulless effort with no meaningful benefit.

Helen also realized that her physical disability was related to her being on the wrong professional path. She saw too that she was overwhelmed with stress. She needed to step off this track and fast.

After several years of this sickness and hitting rock-bottom, I was finally connected with a great behavioral optometrist who diagnosed me as having a binocular disorder, and I got some relief through eye exercises and medication. As I felt a bit better, I realized too that I had to leave this computer job. Once I committed to needing to leave, and to slow down, I found a wonderful part-time job at my son's private school as the school librarian. It's fun, relaxing, stress-free, and I'm working with children and books, and I'm beloved by my colleagues. I just love it. I'm doing what I enjoy, and my eyes and dizziness are so much better. I've let go of the stress, and I'm much happier now.

HELEN'S ADVICE

- Do anything you can to let go of stress. Being on the wrong work path can make you sick.
- Listen to your gut, your intuition—it's right.
- Follow your heart—always.

What great advice Helen gives. Letting go of stress and saying YES! to following your intuition and heart can work miracles. The amazing news for me regarding my health is that I have been tracheitis-free since the day I walked out the door of my last corporate job and chose a new path. No need for antibiotics, no frequent trips to the doctor—the illness is gone, as is the cause of the stress I experienced. I am no longer stuck on a path that is in opposition to who I am. I couldn't agree more with Helen about the importance of letting go of stress. Moving away from work that is wrong for you can save your health and your life.

Hear Your Body

Our bodies communicate, always. From the smallest ailments to the larger forms of malaise or disease, we're receiving continual, vital information from our bodies about the condition of our minds, emotions, and spirits. There are many approaches to understanding the information our bodies share. Vast numbers of helpful resources and tools are available to learn how to decipher our physical messages. From studying the chakra system and energy healing techniques such as reiki to exploring acupuncture, crystal healing, tai chi, meditation, or energy medicine as a whole, we can choose to embark on a lifelong journey of understanding the knowledge our body expresses. Tapping into our body's wisdom, we uncover new ways to heal.

No single approach is best; the key is to find the approach that works for you. For me, studying reiki was instrumental in connecting me with the universal life force energy and flow. Experiencing energy flow in myself and others, and being able to sense energy gaps and stoppages, has been transformational. For others, meditation and learning to be in silent communication with themselves is life-changing. For others still, simply going inward and asking "What is my body telling me?" is helpful.

Whatever your chosen approach, the first step is to accept that your body is indeed communicating. Listening and taking heed is necessary to achieve full health and well-being. By opening our minds to the possibility that our emotional and spiritual blocks contribute to our malaise and disease, we can unlock our potential. We release ourselves from the many mind-forged manacles that keep us chained to our limitations, physical and otherwise.

One easy way to begin to understand your body's messages is to look at your current ailment for a possible metaphoric meaning. What might this ailment be showing you, literally? For instance, if you're having eye problems, as Helen did, what might you need to "see" more clearly about your current situation? In Helen's case, her eyes were literally and figuratively revealing that using her eyes for computer work was not working for her. On a literal level, a librarian must use her eyes for her work, yet Helen was experiencing dizziness and nausea when she used them. Message: Time to consider stopping this job or this type of work. On a metaphoric level, eye problems can mean "What are you not seeing clearly?" Message: You need to see how the stress and joylessness of this work are hurting you.

Exploring your ailment for what it means metaphorically can be quite helpful in revealing where you need to make key changes. I am certainly not suggesting that you abandon traditional medical approaches. On the contrary, I recommend that you explore a range of approaches that feel right to you in addressing your issue. One of those worthwhile approaches involves expanding your view of what your ailment could be telling you, then taking action to address it.

Some examples of possible underlying meanings behind illness follow.

Physical Issue	*Underlying Question or Issue to Consider*
Arm pain/problems	What am I *holding onto* or embracing that needs to be released?
Back pain/problems	Who or what is causing me to bear an *undue burden*?
Bladder or bowel problems	What problems or fears am I carrying that *must be released*?
Digestive problems	What ideas, beliefs, or experiences am I *having trouble digesting*?
Eye pain/problems	What needs to be *seen* that I've ignored?
Fatigue problems	What in life is *wearing me out* and making me sleep or shut off?
Fever problems	In what ways am I *burning up with anger*?
Hearing/ear problems	What am I not *hearing that must be heard*?
Leg pain/problems	In what ways am I not *standing on my own two legs*?
Lung problems	How am I struggling to *breathe in life and experience*?
Neck pain/problems	Who or what is being *a pain in the neck*?
Ovarian problems	What am I *longing to create* that I haven't, or what have I created in my life that I wish to move away from?
Being overweight	What do I fear most, and how am I surrounding myself with layers *to protect me* from what I fear?
Being underweight	How am I rejecting myself, and *refusing to nourish and care* for myself?
Skin problems	How is my *boundary between myself and the world* around me in need of development and strengthening?
Throat pain/problems	What am I not *speaking the truth* about?

A helpful approach to understanding the meaning of your physical ailments is to ask *your intuitive self*, your higher self, to advise you about what this illness could be expressing about your life. When you get into the habit of consulting this dimension of yourself, the information you receive becomes clearer, more directed and pointed each time. It shows you how to adjust your life *now* to alleviate the stress and strain on your body, mind, and spirit.

I have found an extremely beneficial resource in my life and work—Louise Hay's *You Can Heal Your Life*.[1] In this groundbreaking book, Ms. Hay describes many major ailments or diseases that we commonly experience today and reveals a key underlying problem that is potentially at the core of each disease. Use outside tools and resources (including this one) only if the information feels true for you and *compels* you to explore it further.

Understanding that your body is a physical expression of the larger you—your spirit, your life energy, your vibration, your thoughts and emotions—will help you gain a broader perspective and deeper wisdom about what holds you back. You'll see clearly what contributes to your *dis-ease*.

Heed Your Intuition

While our bodies regularly communicate essential information, our intuition is attempting to make itself heard as well. But what it says often falls on deaf ears. Our intuition—the inner wisdom that provides direction and guidance—is a vital part of who we are, yet we often completely disregard it. Western society doesn't yet honor intuition as a source of reliable information, but other, older and wiser cultures do. They revere intuition as a way to connect with the "all that is"—the spiritual, divine, creative force within each of us that binds us to each other and to the universe as a whole. Heeding your intuition will help keep you on a path that is true for you, a path that will prove to be the most fulfilling and satisfying.

The best way I know of to begin hearing your inner voice is to develop a keen awareness of the dialogue that occurs within you. Start by becoming aware of your inner thoughts, and of any physical sensations that accompany these thoughts. Practicing awareness of your intuitive voice helps you access your own, best guidance, which has your true interests at heart.

The second step is to find regular times to calm your body and still your mind. This practice can be done through meditation, deep breathing, yoga, exercise, gardening, painting—any activity that focuses your attention and quiets the chatter of your mind. In this way, you "drop down" to a deeper place in your body, where intuition can be accessed more easily. Your intuition and inner voice is your guide to identifying and moving toward what you truly long to be in this lifetime. Various guided-meditation CDs (I highly recommend Shakti Gawain's *Creative Visualization Meditations*[2]) and books, including *Developing Intuition*[3] by Shakti Gawain, can help you on this path.

If you don't heed your intuition, you're rudderless. Life will unfold as it will, but you will suffer more than you need to without your inner guidance. By using your intuition and inner wisdom to direct you, your life will proceed more smoothly, positively, and constructively. Heeding your intuition helps you stay "in the flow" of who you naturally are.

Another way of getting in touch with your intuition is to continually ask yourself questions and listen to the answers. Begin to foster an ongoing inner dialogue with yourself, and use your inner experience as your highest authority. Get used to accessing and integrating your gut instinct in all you do. Honor and abide by your hunches. You will be amazed at what opens up for you, and what suffering you'll avoid when you do. Start by asking your higher self "yes" or "no" questions at first, and follow the guidance you receive. Then, little by little, go inside, ask for guidance, and use this wisdom as your highest authority for everything you do.

Follow Your Heart

What keeps us from doing what we want to, long to, need to, in order to be happy and thrive? Each of us needs to ask ourselves this pivotal question every day, every week, every year: *What holds me back from following my heart?*

If we examine the answers people most commonly give to this question, the responses fall into several categories. *Fear* is the first and biggest deterrent to following our hearts. "What if I fail and make a fool of myself?" people say. "Won't they think I'm selfish and egotistical to follow these dreams?" is another common question. And another major fear: "Will I be harmed or become more vulnerable if I follow my heart?"

We're afraid of following our hearts because doing so might bring us to a place where we'll:

- Leave others behind
- Make others jealous, angry, or resentful of us
- Appear greater than someone else
- Be forced to face our own uniqueness
- Have to move out of our comfort zones
- Be led to make a huge leap of faith
- Become more vulnerable to scrutiny and criticism
- See that we are truly capable of achieving our dreams, which can feel overwhelming

So what's so scary about achieving our dreams? What intimidates many of us is that if we are really capable of achieving our dreams, then nothing is holding us back but *ourselves*, and that idea overwhelms many people. A friend of mine said: "You mean, this is all in my hands? I think I'd rather stay comforted in the idea that there are things outside of my control that are holding me back."

No, it's not *all* in our hands. But one thing surely is—the ability and need to follow our hearts. We were given these longings for the experience of following them, not denying that they exist or thinking that we have to revise them. When we ignore the longings of our hearts, sickness often comes.

The second biggest reason we don't follow our hearts is that *we are told not to.* In our society, we focus almost exclusively on external barometers of health, happiness, and success. We disregard or degrade the inner criteria that our hearts yearn to use to define success and joy, such as feeling valued, loved, peaceful, nurturing, stress-free, worthwhile, and of service. You can't see or hold these by-products of a successful life, but to many, they are the most precious. Most often we are told not to follow our hearts by people who have failed to do so. Following your heart requires stretching. It takes you out of your comfort zone and demands courage, fortitude, and faith. But those who do follow their hearts are the most expansive, inspiring, and exciting people you will ever meet.

Hundreds of people have told me that they have been advised by loved ones, friends, and colleagues to "do the safe thing," "stop living pipe dreams," and "grow up and face facts." Such misguided advice tells you to live less than who you are.

MOVING FORWARD TO BREAKTHROUGH

✳ STEP BACK

Since you have chosen to read this book, you are probably undergoing a significant change in your work and life—one that is challenging, exciting, and frightening. Or perhaps you are longing to make a dramatic change and seek support and guidance to make it.

Take this opportunity to open your mind and your heart. Allow in a new perspective, a keener ability to connect with your higher level of information and insight. Embrace a broader, more positive interpretation about the situation you're experiencing.

This step, of allowing in a deeper understanding of *what is*, requires:

- Believing in the *possibility* that this life situation has been co-created by you for your own happiness and expansion
- Being willing to see new interpretations of old, negative patterns that are longing to be released
- Embracing the idea that your moving forward now, while perhaps discomforting, will be rewarding and enriching

Think about the situation that is causing you the most distress in your life at this time. In your journal, capture all your thoughts. *No censoring, please—write everything that comes to mind.*

- What *exactly* is causing you pain?
- What and who does it involve? (Family, children, professional life, moving, loss of a loved one or of a role you have played, a new role or function, a conflict, a failure, etc.)
- Flesh out as fully as possible all aspects and dimensions of this situation or transition.
- What are you telling yourself about your competence, worthiness, and abilities when you think about this situation? How are you beating yourself up?
- What are you most afraid of, or worried or concerned about?

✳ **LET GO** of ignoring or resisting *what is*.

- What are you *resisting* that your heart says it wants?
- What are you *ignoring* that won't go away?
- What potential options are you *rejecting* that may be partly acceptable to you, but you've "thrown them out with the bathwater"?

Once you become clear about what you are ignoring and resisting, take this step: *Embrace* what you are resisting. If it's that you hate your work, embrace that reality. If it's that you're ill all the time, face that reality. If it's that you can't take the stress of your life anymore, see that—and commit to doing one small thing about it, this week.

What I will no longer ignore is: _____

The step I will take to face what I'm resisting and get help to address it is: _____

_____

✳ **SAY YES!** to hearing the messages of your body, your intuition, and your heart.

Recommended Steps

1. Take several down-to-your-stomach, diaphragmatic breaths. (For a wonderful guide to deep and meditative breathing, check out *Three Deep Breaths*,[4] by Thomas Crum.)
2. Bring to mind the physical ailment you're suffering from. Fully feel it in your body and think of its impact on your life.
3. Now quietly go inward and ask yourself—consult your inner guidance, your intuition—to tell you everything about this ailment.

- What does my ailment really represent?
- What must I *say yes!* to for this ailment to be healed?
- What does my heart tell me to do right now?

4. Ask yourself, "What one step can I take this month to honor my intuitive voice, follow my heart, and heal this ailment?" Write down the answer, and commit to taking this one small step this month.

5. Write in your journal what you experience as you *Let Go* of what you are resisting, and *Say Yes!* to your body, intuition, and heart.

Remember

You are meant to listen to your body, follow your heart, and heed your intuition, not deny them. You will heal.

Helen reminds us

"See yourself two years from now, and imagine what your life can be. Don't give up on yourself; keep focusing on what you need to do to feel better. You will get through this."

✳ **BREAKTHROUGH** "I am healthy and strong."

5

Overcoming Loss

We are shaped and fashioned
by what we love.

JOHANN WOLFGANG VON GOETHE

✳ **STEP BACK TO EXPLORE** Grieving lost parts of yourself.

✳ **LET GO** of overidentifying with one aspect.

✳ **SAY YES!** to healing lost parts of yourself.

✳ **BREAKTHROUGH**
"I am integrated and whole."

✳ **Natalie:** *I built my career to a high level, and I was in a very senior role that affected many people. In the beginning, I generally liked my work, but throughout the years I did have an inkling—a strong one—that perhaps this wasn't the right focus or professional life for me. I'd have conversations with other people at my level about the downsides of being the "master or mistress of the universe"—of working so many hours, of not being able to see my son's Little League games, of being handcuffed to our laptops while on vacation. We explored the notion that "there must be a better way." But I never stopped to figure out what that could be for me. And then something happened that changed everything.*

My boss was a woman my age, and she was gifted at her work. Sally inspired people, helped them be all they could be. I'd worked with her for years, and we'd forged a deep friendship. We also shared respect and appreciation for each other, which was somewhat rare among my counterparts. She had worked for the company for thirty years and was very respected as a major contributor. She was preparing for her long-awaited retirement and was excited about moving to Florida with her husband, now that their kids were grown and doing well. She'd tell me about looking forward to walking on the beach, playing tennis, and just enjoying life and relishing time with her husband. And then it happened. Three weeks before her retirement, Sally was diagnosed with lung cancer. And she was dead thirteen weeks later. Here was someone my age whom my coworkers and I had loved, revered, who'd made a huge difference in all our lives and for the company. And she was gone.

It was a cataclysmic loss for me and for the senior team. But even more devastating was that our company didn't do a thing to help us deal with our loss. Nothing—no support, no time to mourn, no avenue to express our grief and despair—not a thing was done to

---

✳ Natalie (not her real name) is a 52-year-old senior executive at a Fortune 500 company.

acknowledge how deeply we were all suffering, or to help us come to grips with the immense hole Sally's passing left in our lives.

Something happened to me then. A complete upheaval—a mental, physical, and spiritual upheaval, followed by what I call a "fundamental transition." A voice inside me kept saying, "This could have been you, Natalie. If you had thirteen weeks to live, would you say that you're happy, satisfied with what you are doing?" I realized that I'd have to answer this question with a resolute "NO," and that scared me. On top of it all, the company I'd given my life to completely let me down. I was disillusioned and devastated by its coldness. I knew then that things would never be the same for me.

Natalie was devastated at losing her beloved friend and mentor to untimely death. Her boss Sally not only stood for all things important and positive in Natalie's mind but also mirrored Natalie herself. She shared many critical characteristics with Natalie: her age, her occupation, her years of dedication to the company, her innate desire to help others, and her years of personal sacrifice to make a difference at work. Losing Sally so suddenly was a terrible shock, in part because it reminded Natalie that her own days are not infinite. This type of wake-up call creates an urgency to act. But it wasn't just the sadness of losing Sally that spurred Natalie to action. It was the heartbreaking disillusionment she experienced watching her revered company fall from grace. It was the realization that the entity to which she'd given pieces of her life no longer deserved her selfless dedication. Natalie realized in a flash that parts of herself had been lost for years, and she wanted them back.

After grieving about Sally's death and my feelings of loss for a long while, I came to realize that being the "mistress of the universe" was no longer important to me. What I really loved to do was help people develop and watch them grow. I wanted to coach, not tell. Key parts of me—compassion, service, and caregiving—had been unfulfilled over the years. Increasingly in the corporate world, coldness was replacing compassion, bottom-line goal attainment was replacing service. Compassion was considered "emotional" or "soft" and unwelcome in the corporate role I played. My internal debate grew louder and louder. I asked myself, "Do I want money, prestige, power and influence, and material comfort, or do I want to be known for helping people grow?" I became aware that my struggle to remain on top and to meet the continual demands of overt and covert corporate mandates had kept me from being a compassionate coach, a true service provider, and a developer of people.

The Wake-Up Call of Losing a Loved One

Why is losing someone we love from an untimely death such a wake-up call, as it was for Natalie? Reasons for this are numerous, but most powerful is the realization that what you count on in life is, in fact, an illusion. We expect so many things during our lives—our health will be good, we'll live a long and productive life, our children will love and honor us, our employer will treat us well, our dreams will come true, and we'll get what we deserve. But when a traumatic event occurs, it often shatters our illusions and expectations. It makes us aware that all of these expectations, these things we count on, are simply creations of our minds and hearts. They are expectations based on hopes. That doesn't mean we shouldn't dream—of course we should. In fact, keeping our dreams and longings ever-present and front-and-center in our lives helps guide us to move forward.

But counting on something outside yourself as *inevitable* and believing that you are in complete control causes suffering. When you count too heavily on outside things—events, people, jobs, money, and possessions—to bring you joy, fulfillment, and a sense of security, a wake-up call will surely push you toward another path, a more grounded and self-affirming way of living that honors who you are at your core.

A sudden loss of a loved one reminds us that nothing in life is permanent, and that there are no guarantees. Loss also illustrates that life will continually deliver experiences that offer you opportunities to grow and shift positively. But many of these experiences may not be enjoyable or comfortable. Truly expansive experiences are often the most challenging. Suffering from loss reminds you that the future life you picture may not necessarily come to pass, not because you don't deserve joy and success, but because what you've attached to so strongly could be limiting you.

Losing Parts of Yourself

Grieving the loss of something or someone you love or identify with strongly also points to mourning losses within yourself—parts of you that have gone underground to survive or to succeed on the path you've chosen.

When I was laid off from my final senior corporate position, I felt that in a sense it was a death. I realized, once and for all, that the corporate identity I had clung too so desperately—a powerful "mistress of the universe" identity—was a sham because I had been forced to give up so much of myself in order to keep it. I was an impostor, and I suffered trying to behave in ways that weren't truly me. The confident, compassionate, inspiring leader in me was gone, replaced by an insecure bully. My humor, sense of play, creativity, and joy had been snuffed out, as I marshalled all my resources for years to survive what felt like a living hell.

This false professional self was all I knew at the time, and losing it was daunting. The loss forced me to wake up and accept that I would have to reclaim other dimensions of myself. I realized I needed to create a totally new life and professional identity. In her grieving process, Natalie realized that she had lost parts of herself she wanted to recover—namely, as a caregiver, nuturer, service-giver, and compassionate developer of people. Interestingly, after Sally's death, Natalie also suddenly needed to help her mother recover from a devastating stroke, which required a tremendous amount of time and energy. In addition, Natalie's son, who suffers from a severe learning disability, needed more care and dedication than Natalie could provide if she continued on her high-powered path. All of these considerations created a deep need for change. Natalie embraced this need, putting into motion significant life change.

Natalie found the courage to request a six-month sabbatical to give her the space and time to rethink her life. She stepped off the fast track, into a more awake, aware, and self-affirming direction. Slowly but surely she worked to recover key aspects of herself that had gone underground. After her sabbatical, she decided to return to work on a part-time basis for the corporation, allowing her to meet important financial obligations in a role that serves her professional needs of being productive and collaborating in a positive way with other business people.

She also relocated with her family to another state that provides her son with greater educational and developmental opportunities. She and her husband, who previously were "moving on separate but parallel tracks," are now building a new house together, which serves as a "wonderful creative outlet and bonding experience for us and our marriage." They're now on the same path, heading in the same direction. Natalie is dedicating a great deal of time and care to finding the right higher education institution for her teenage son, one that will help him continue on his path of development and self-reliance. In doing so, she has become very active in understanding and advocating for the needs of disabled children. In her own way, Natalie is forging new territory in exposing and addressing the severe lack of high-quality special needs programs and services for young adults nationwide.

Natalie says of her life now: *I'm still not exactly sure where I'll end up professionally, but I'm truly enjoying this process of self-discovery. My life is very different now; it allows me to focus on several different yet important aspects of who I am, not just the one—the corporate self. It's unlocked my compassion and love and need of being of service to others, and allowed me to be very comfortable with these important dimensions, instead of suppressing or denying them. I think that I'm finally happy in the realization that now is the time for me to be fully available for my son and my husband, and help them develop and grow as individuals. It's interesting, I've gone from telling people what to do to saying, "Please just let me know if and when I can be of help." I can see the enormous difference that approach makes, and it's powerful. Overall, it's a very good life; I feel blessed and useful, and my blood pressure is lower than it's ever been!*

NATALIE'S ADVICE

- Take time to think about how you want to integrate and bring forward *everything* that matters to you in life (work, family, marriage, children, passions, experiences, abilities, yearnings, etc.).
- Avoid overidentifying with one aspect of yourself. Make sure you honor the many dimensions of who you are.
- Don't make the same mistake I did. If you're looking for a "better way," find it now. Don't wait.

Bring Forward What Matters to You

Many dimensions make up who you are. Some of these aspects, over time, become suppressed in order for you to gain approval, fit in, or be viewed as an accepted member of the tribe. Often what you suppress in your professional life now is what you needed to suppress in your childhood, to receive love and care. Now is the time to break away from the herd and become aware of the parts of yourself you've pushed underground.

For some, being compassionate and caregiving has to be downplayed in the work environment in order to succeed, as Natalie experienced. For others, being gifted intuitively is the hidden attribute. For me, my "emotional" or "soft" side and my people and relationship skills were seen as a detriment in my highly male, competitive work environment.

In today's corporate culture, pure, unbridled creativity is sometimes considered a negative. While many women are employed in creative fields such as advertising, publishing, and the arts, I've heard senior-level corporate managers say that "creative" individuals have less business savvy. As a consequence, individuals sometimes temper creativity and "out-of-the-box thinking" so as not to be seen as lacking in business sense.

Spirituality and a desire to contribute meaningfully often get suppressed at work. Those who don't share these longings can be disparaging about altruistic and philanthropic goals, ridiculing them as "pie in the sky" pipe dreams. In my seminars about finding fulfillment in professional life, I've heard people say, "Sure, that's all well and good to want to do something meaningful, but is it practical? After all, I have to pay the mortgage." Other qualities that individuals often push underground to fit in are humor and playfulness, expressiveness, adventurousness, devotion to family, sensitivity to others, loyalty, integrity, honesty, courage to challenge the status quo, and the ability to stand up for one's rights and the rights of others.

In the process of recovering from loss, it's important to look closely at the parts of you that have been suppressed at work, in your family, and among your peers. What are you longing to show others that has been hidden for years?

Review the list below, and circle any aspects of you or your ideal life that have been suppressed in order for you to gain acceptance and approval, or simply to survive your current situation.

Adventure/Excitement
Beauty/Aesthetics
Being Catalyst for Action/Change
Competition/Excelling
Creativity/Imagination/Innovation
Devotion to Family and Others Outside Work
Discovery/Learning
Emotional Intelligence
Flexibility
Freedom/Independence
Glamour/Prestige
Healthful Living

Humor

Influencing Others

Integrity/Truth

Intellectual Stimulation

Intuitive Thinking

Kindness/Empathy/Compassion

Knowledge

Leadership/Managing Others

Loyalty/Dependability

Mastery/Achievement

Mental or Intellectual Challenge

Moral/Ethical Fulfillment

Order/Balance

Performing/Creative Arts

Physical Fitness or Prowess

Playfulness/Fun

Pleasure

Power/Authority

Precision

Recognition

Respect

Risk-Taking

Security

Service to Others

Service to the World

Social Connection and Relatedness

Sensuality

Spirituality

Standing Up for Your/Others' Rights

Stability

Teaching

Teamwork/Working with Others

Tranquility/Peace

Which of these dimensions of you or your ideal life that you circled above would you most like to bring forward today? Begin by choosing two or three.

_____

_____

_____

Avoid Overidentification with One Aspect

Natalie reminds us to avoid focusing on just one dimension of yourself. I couldn't agree more. My experience bears this out as well. The day after I was laid off from my corporate job, I didn't know what to do with myself. I set the alarm for six a.m., got up, put on a suit, had a quick breakfast, and slipped quietly out of the house, as I'd always done. Except this time, I had nowhere to go. I drove about aimlessly and ended up in the parking lot of a Starbucks. I sat there for hours, my head in my hands, dazed and confused, wondering what I was to do now. I simply couldn't face my children or our children's caregiver, and tell them the truth . . . not yet. My husband knew, but I couldn't face him either. I was utterly lost. I didn't know who I was without my big corporate job.

As I aimlessly drove around for the next few weeks, I saw things I had never seen before in the light of day in my hometown. It was a revelation. I thought to myself, "My God, there are so many people who *don't* live the corporate life—who don't leave at seven in the morning and return at seven at night, who have interesting stores and unique businesses, creative or artistic products to sell and fascinating things to do." It was a shock to see how much went on in my community that had nothing to do with corporate life. I was relieved and overjoyed. I thought to myself, "Perhaps I could make a go of another kind of life after all." Finally, after several weeks, I regrouped and refocused, and discovered a different profession I wanted to pursue. At a nearby university I began studying marriage and family therapy, which gave me an exciting new direction to delve into, a new identity to form.

A critical lesson to learn is that each of us is much more than one function, one job, one role. You are a rich, multifaceted, and complex individual with an enormous array of diverse talents and abilities, all wanting expression. This is not an "either/or" life—this is an "everything" life. With focus, energy, and commitment, you can bring forth all of the aspects of yourself that you love and wish to honor and develop. This is not only possible but necessary, to live a full, satisfying, and joyful life.

An easy way to determine aspects you may have lost touch with and wish to bring forward involves a quick exercise. Ask yourself:

- What talents and abilities did you have as a young child and teen that made you deeply happy when you focused on them?
- What did you used to do in your childhood and early teens that made you feel "in the flow"—joyful, expansive, special, wonderful?
- What things did you do as a child and young adult that made time fly by, making hours pass like seconds?

Often what we are gifted at and loved doing as children represents special talents we still possess that are wanting expression. Some of us are wonderful at making friends and having fun parties. Others create beautiful designs and objects. Others somehow know how to build amazing engineering masterpieces in their backyard with only clay, sticks, and chicken wire. Still others sing beautiful, breathtaking songs.

What were your special gifts and abilities as a child, and are you using these gifts in your current life?

Find a "Better Way" Now

Like Natalie, many professional women say to themselves continually, under their breath, "There must be a better way." What about you? Do you utter this statement to yourself on a regular basis? I did.

For me, a better way in life meant not going to an office every day, spending more time with my family, having more control over what I do and when I do it, being of service to others, and creating and designing my own ideas and programs, rather than executing others'. I now live this better way, and I can't believe I waited so long to accept that I could.

Natalie's better way meant being more available for her family, bringing forward her compassion and wish to serve others, dedicating more time to endeavors that are meaningful to her, and finding new avenues for her son's development that will increase his self-reliance for the rest of his life. Not bad for a better way!

Following Natalie's advice, let's take this opportunity to help you find your better way. What does that mean to you? Take some time to ponder what "a better way" would look like for your life. Think out of the box. Be creative and expansive. Don't limit yourself to "how's" right now; explore your thoughts with no worry about the mechanics. First you have to determine what your "better way" looks like before you can build it.

Ask yourself, "What would my better way look like now?" In your journal, outline it in detail.

Don't Wait to Change Your Life

Natalie also urges us, "Don't wait." How often have you heard a story that illustrates that "waiting until _____" (retirement, or after the kids go to college, or when this project is over, or when you have more vacation time) is simply waiting too long. I believe that your deep longings and dreams are to be honored and heeded, not as a "I'll do it when _____" but as a guidepost for what to do *now*. What you dream of points to what you find most meaningful, joyful, and enriching to you. Dream now and move toward your dream; don't wait.

The story of my dear friend and colleague Mike Jaffe is the most powerful example I've ever heard of the impact of not waiting, of taking positive action in your life now. In fact, it's so powerful that Mike calls himself the Human Wake-Up Call and dedicates his life and work to helping others take vital steps to wake up to their own lives.[1]

Like so many others, I never played a very active role in where my career was headed. The promotions and job changes kept coming, so I simply "floated down the river," letting life take me from one place to another. None of it truly felt like it was my "right" work. I was unhappy, but moderately comfortable.

Several years ago, my floating "river" took me to another Fortune 500 company, and I found myself in yet another meaningless job. I had just moved to Connecticut from New York City, and my commute increased from twenty-five minutes to more than two hours each way. Each morning my wife would drive me to the station with our one-year-old daughter sleeping in back. I'd come home each night and my little girl would be exactly as I left her, fast asleep in her car seat. Days would go by where I wouldn't see her awake at all. Seeing her almost only when she was asleep reminded me that this was not the kind of parent I wanted to be, absent from her waking world.

I found myself wishing away my weekdays, hoping for each one to finish sooner than the clock would allow. I realized that my work felt unimportant to me yet again, and I didn't know what to do about it. I was our family's sole financial provider, and I didn't know what would fulfill me. I had no direction. So I did what many people do—nothing. I just kept floating downstream and time kept slipping by.

Then, one Monday afternoon, I was sitting outside my office having lunch. As I sat basking in the sun, I looked up at my office building and was overcome by the sense that it controlled my life. I realized at that moment that I HAD to make a change . . . even if it was a small change. I had to take action.

So I decided that the next morning, instead of rushing to catch the early train, I would take a later train so I could have breakfast with my wife and daughter. I remember smiling, thinking this was a good first step. Not a big step, but at least a new beginning. So the next day, despite my concerns that perhaps I should just get on the early train after all, we spent a wonderful time having breakfast together. It was a beautiful morning. After breakfast, my wife dropped me off and I took the train into New York City, smiling the whole way. I felt I had some control of my life, and it felt wonderful.

I got on the subway, and instead of being in my office, I was underground at 8:45 a.m. when the first plane slammed into the North Tower of the World Trade Center, into my floor, hitting my desk, and killing almost every single member of my group, including my boss and team—300 colleagues I worked with and friends I valued deeply, each with their own dreams, their own beautiful families. The morning I had breakfast with my family was September 11, 2001.

Mike's story reminds us that we're not in control, and attempting to be in complete control is futile. Instead, we need to wake up to what matters most to us, and live from that understanding, each day, every day, as fully, deeply, and passionately as we can. Doing so creates a life well lived.

Mike says of his life now: *Today I am a business and personal leadership coach, sharing my message and empowering others through coaching, mentoring, seminars, and keynote speaking. I have been blessed to have touched people across the U.S., in Canada, Europe, and even as far away as Nigeria. I love my family and my life as much as ever (including my son, who has since been born). Now, I even love my work. I wonder how I lived any other way for so long.*

Now is the time for you to step forward and create the life you want. Don't wait.

MOVING FORWARD TO BREAKTHROUGH

✳ **STEP BACK**

Visualizing the Integrated You

Close your eyes, and take three long, deep breaths. Bring to mind an image of the overidentified part of you. What does it look like? What is it wearing, doing, holding? In your mind's eye, walk toward this part/individual with your arms outstretched. Embrace it with love. Ask it to tell you what it has been working so hard to give you. Listen carefully, and then offer your deepest thanks.

Now visualize the new part of you that you wish to bring forward. What does it look like? See it clearly. Ask it to step forward into a circle with you and the overidentified part. Embrace each other. Ask the new part what it would like to bring forward in your life. Listen carefully. Offer your deepest thanks.

Now ask the two parts their permission to work together, to collaborate and support each other, so that they can help each other achieve what each desires and needs. Ask them to avoid sabotaging each other or becoming overly possessive of you. Ask them for their help to be more balanced and integrated.

Listen to what they say. Hear what they would like to give, receive, and achieve in collaboration. Offer your deepest thanks.

Visualize the two parts leaving the circle slowly, walking away together, hand in hand, as caring and supportive friends who are relieved and excited at being able to work together rather than compete for your attention.

Write in your journal all that you experienced in this exercise of healing the lost parts of yourself, how you have *Let Go* of overidentifying with a single part of yourself.

✴ **LET GO** of overidentifying with one aspect of yourself.

Think about the situation that is causing you the most distress at this time. Using your journal, capture all your thoughts. *No censoring, please—write everything that comes to mind.*

- What aspect of you are you currently *overidentifying* with?
- How does this overidentification consume or limit you? Flesh out as fully as possible all the ways you have overidentified with this role or aspect.
- What positive things does this overidentified part give you? (What are the benefits of overidentification?)
- What are the costs you have to pay to overidentify with this part?
- What are the risks of letting this part become less dominant and bringing other parts forward?

Ask yourself, "What one step can I take this month to let go of overidentifying with just one part of myself?" Write down the answer, and commit to taking this one small step this month.

✴ **SAY YES!** to healing lost parts of yourself.

Recommended Steps

1. Allow yourself to feel loss.

   Many people experiencing loss or trauma are afraid to allow themselves to truly *feel* this experience at all levels. Feeling our emotions fully can be frightening, since we are socialized to consider deep emotion somehow "wrong" or "weak."

   Pressured by peers, family, and society to "get over it" or "get a life and move on," many don't allow themselves to feel the pain, sadness, fear, and regret, of their current situation. But if you deny yourself the full experience of feelings associated with your situation, you stay stuck. Fully experiencing loss allows you to see clearly what you want to reclaim.

2. Quietly go inward and ask yourself—consult your inner guidance, your intuition—to tell you:

- What parts of you are you mourning the loss of?
- What do you miss in your life that you want back?
- What emotions do you feel when thinking about these missing parts?
- What aspects of you or your life do you want to bring forward now?

Take out your journal, and write down what your intuitive voice and heart have shared. Review the information. Allow it to soak in.

3. Ask yourself, "What one step can I take this month to heal and bring forward lost parts of myself that I miss?" Write down the answer, and commit to taking this one small step this month.

Remember

You are a multifaceted individual. Your life is a lovely mosaic, with many patterns, colors, and dimensions that enhance each other. Avoid overidentification with any one role, function, or aspect of yourself, and remember how richly varied you are.

Natalie reminds us

"It's okay to still be searching for what you'd eventually love to do professionally. But in the meantime, live life fully as you are, not as a pretender. I've found it's very freeing to bring forward my compassion, service, and caregiving longings, and to be comfortable finally in offering these gifts to others."

✳ **BREAKTHROUGH** "I am integrated and whole."

6

Achieving
Self-Love

Know thyself.

SOCRATES

EMPOWERMENT WITH SELF

* **STEP BACK TO EXPLORE** Needing to reclaim your power from a source outside of you.

* **LET GO** of giving up your power to others or things.

* **SAY YES!** to acting in alignment with the *real* you.

* **BREAKTHROUGH**
"I love and accept myself."

* **Marsha:** *My personal story is full of bumps and challenges. When I was young, my mom died, and there was a bitter custody battle for me between my father and my mother's relatives. I ended up living with distant relatives, and it was a very unhappy situation. I was neglected and ignored, and life was bleak for me. In my teens, I experienced sexual abuse at the hands of a trusted family friend. All of this contributed to my sense that I had very little power or control in my life. I think I had the expectation that what was coming down the pike for me in life was going to be a tough struggle. I was surrounded by misogyny and chauvinism as a young person, which forged in me a strong sense of feminism that remains with me today. Unlike the men who surrounded me, the women in my life were caring, nurturing, and very powerful. I grew to believe that women in general were strong, competent, emotionally intelligent and resilient, and in some ways even superior to men, and I set out to prove it.*

In my professional life, I followed the path of demonstrating that I could do what men could do, and better. I went to college, got a good job after graduating, attended business school at night, then began pursuing employment in marketing and management. All of this was mostly about making money and gaining power and responsibility. My driving need to prove that I was invulnerable and self-sufficient, and my anger at having to do so fueled me all along the way. During my twenties and early thirties, I found my work somewhat enjoyable and interesting, collaborating with smart people I liked, working toward developing and launching high-quality products. But as time wore on, the work and my experiences grew less and less satisfying or positive, and my anger ignited. Trauma and disillusionment ensued, job after job—terrible leaders and managers, the company's insa-

---

* Marsha (not her real name) is a 48-year-old vice president of marketing turned social worker.

tiable need for growth that couldn't be sustained, and relentless changes in organizational structure in futile attempts to achieve the impossible. I felt like I was the little boy in the story "The Emperor's New Clothes" over and over again, where I'd be viewed as too negative each time I told it like it was at work. I continued doing this work mostly for the security that came from a large, steady paycheck, great benefits, and being associated with some top marketing organizations.

Honestly speaking, I hated what I did for a living, and who I'd become, as a manager and employee, for quite a long time. I shut down, and I lost touch with my creative, nurturing, powerful, and resilient aspects. What emerged instead were the battle scars of years of feeling false, unsupported, and cynical. I was tough on others, overly sensitive, disdainful of my peers and bosses, and rageful at having to race around executing what seemed to be doomed endeavors. Despite some strong professional "wins," I had lost respect for who I was at work.

Then I was fired, and truthfully, I should have been. I said to myself then, "C'mon, Marsha, what are you doing? You really need to find work you don't hate." I went through some deep soul-searching then, took time off to reflect, restore, disentangle from my past. I needed to find the energy to create a new life based on who I wanted to be. I thought, "You've spent half your life doing work you don't respect—you have to find something you love."

In my home life, I had faced a tough divorce and was a single parent raising a young child. I love my son deeply, and wanted with all my heart to provide him not only stability and security, but also a role model of loving life and loving who you are and what you stand up for. After being fired, I woke up and said, "This is it . . . I have to make a change." I engaged in a period of deep thought and exploration through a variety of avenues (therapy, yoga, retreats, energy work, study, etc.). I emerged committed to a new direction. I decided to pursue a career in social work, and I haven't looked back since.

Marsha's story is one of struggling to remain connected to her "real" self, the essential self that is hopeful, resilient, creative, positive, and powerful, in the face of crushing experiences that suppressed her spirit. Due to the loss of her mother and the trauma from sexual abuse and subsequent challenging life events, she developed a deep need to protect herself in adult life and find ways to feel invulnerable, safe, and in control. In her effort to feel powerful, though, she moved away from trusting and honoring her inner strength and core abilities. Instead, she moved toward attaining power through outer attachments, such as a powerful job, a large paycheck, and associations with others who made her feel superior. But she hated who she'd become because she had moved in a direction that was antithetical to her "real" self and her core values and beliefs.

Hating What You Do and Who You Have Become

Hating what you do and who you've become means one thing: you've given over your power to something or someone outside yourself. You're acting in ways that are false to who you really are because you think you have to.

In my last years as a corporate professional, I had moments of "realness," with laughter, joy, authenticity, and creativity, but by and large I felt that I could not reveal the person I was inside. I felt I needed to act the part (and it did seem like theater to me) of a ruthless negotiator, a hard-driving manager, a work-obsessed employee, and a follow-the-party-line minion. When a senior executive who had been supportive of me was fired in a humiliating way, my new boss asked me, "So how do you feel about that?" I knew there was only one acceptable answer, so I said, "Fine." Another lie.

Why do we tolerate situations that force us to be inauthentic? Because we feel we have to in order to continue reaping the benefits of our falseness, which are typically about power, security, and safety. We don't realize that anything that drives us to be false is, in fact, maintaining our own powerlessness. If you can't be real at work, you can't be the master of your own life; someone or something else will rule you. If you can't be authentic and truthful, you'll end up living someone else's life, not your own. And you won't like where it takes you.

Discover Where You Are Being False

How can you step away from inauthenticity and begin to like again who you are and what you do? First, you need to recognize when you are feeling false, and understand how and why it's occurring. Explore all of the areas that represent a poor fit with who you are and what you value. Determine where the disconnect lies between the "real" you and this false self. Is it in how you deal with others, and how you make them feel? Does it involve how you manage your power and authority? Or perhaps there is a wide gap between what you truly value and what you're focusing on in your job or life. Perhaps, too, the falseness lies in the way you are behaving, as someone who has no control or power when you know in your heart you do.

My sense of falseness as a corporate professional centered around the type of person I wanted to be at work—loyal, caring, intelligent, calm, truthful, and nurturing. This characterization felt in stark contrast to how others wanted me to be—disloyal, backstabbing, inconstant, reactive, biting, and autocratic. In exploring how I hated what I'd become, I discovered that working for organizations that focus on selling rather than on providing valuable services for people was a terrible fit for me.

Marsha also saw that working with people she didn't respect, on projects that were ill-advised and doomed to fail, was false to her. She hated that she couldn't speak up, and she hated even more working with people who didn't want her to speak up. Subconsciously, these crushing patterns seemed like a repeat from her childhood. Feeling angry and superior all the time exhausted her, draining all her energy and hope that she could find work that felt right.

How did Marsha find the way out? At first, she didn't. She was forced out, fired from her job. But as she admits, she should have been let go, given how she felt about the company and the work. She then did something transformational: she stopped working for a while, drawing on savings and the money she'd received from her severance package. As scary as not being employed and taking time off was, she did it. She removed herself from the pressure and strain of working simply for the paycheck. She stopped in her tracks, took stock, soul-searched, and chose a new direction. Social work as a vocation called to her, and she elected to begin studying new work that would be instrumental in helping others overcome challenge. For Marsha, advocating for others and standing up for those who feel vulnerable, confused, and alone is a work path and identity that finally feels right.

Marsha says of her life now: *I love what I do now, listening deeply to people, making a difference in their lives. I'm able to be there as a needed advocate, someone who can help them feel safe, protected, and supported. I have a goal, an ultimate vision for my life now that excites me. I can see myself in a full private practice, happily married, being a great mother, and writing a book that helps others. I realize now how little I had expected to love what I was doing for a living. But now I know that I can have a career that creates joy for myself and makes a positive difference in the lives of others. Life remains a mystery to me, but I do believe my purpose for being here has to do with being a force of good somehow. I'm much happier following a path that represents hope and possibility rather than pursuing meaningless work for money and security. I want to be true to the more positive and powerful aspects of myself now and act from a belief in goodness and ease rather than in struggle. I love where I am now, and I don't care about other people scratching their heads over the decisions I've made. I make much less money now, but I can say I really like myself and am proud of who I am and what I'm doing, and what I'm being for my son.*

MARSHA'S ADVICE

- If you feel like you can't be honest, truthful, and authentic in your life and work (like you're living in the story "The Emperor's New Clothes"), figure out how your life is false for you. Start finding the "real" you, and be more honest and real in what you say, and in the decisions you make and actions you take.
- Explore where you feel powerless in life and where you are seeking to find power. If you think money or someone else will give you security or power, think again. Find the power within yourself.
- Take needed time out (a day, a week, a month if you can) from the false aspects of your life. Disentangle from your struggle long enough to get some perspective that you don't have to keep being false in order to get your needs met.

Reconnect with the "Real" You

Feeling false means knowing in your heart and soul that what you are saying and doing and how you are behaving is not aligned with what is true for you. You can love and accept yourself only when you are being true to yourself. Women often second-guess themselves. If they are in a situation that feels wrong, they believe *they're* wrong. Moving away from living falsely means understanding from this moment forward that you're not wrong, you're right! What you want to say and do is most likely what needs to be said and done. What you want to do in life is undoubtedly a direction worthy of your exploration and pursuit. If you can't say and be what you want to today, it usually means one of two things. Either you're in the wrong situation and need a change. Or you would benefit from gaining greater access to your inner courage, power, and self-trust, to feel good about being real and to know that you can deal with the consequences.

Find the Power Inside You

Trauma happens. Many women have experienced extreme diminishment and suppression. In our attempts to survive our families and life circumstances, most of us have learned unfortunate lessons that forced us to move away from honoring and believing in ourselves. But to live life fully from this day forward, it is critical that you re-frame these experiences and find their positive meaning. You gleaned beneficial, life-affirming lessons from these experiences, not just negative ones. Marsha did this, for example, by turning her childhood adversity into a deep resolve to help those who are disadvantaged or in need of advocacy and support. Identifying the positive meaning and benefit behind your experiences will help you reconnect with—and unleash—the power that exists within you.

You have great creative power. All that holds us back from accessing this power is our lack of awareness of it. I've witnessed firsthand the miracles that occur when people realize they have learned something powerful and important from their life ex-periences that in turn can be beneficial to others. They realize, based on what they've already survived and accomplished, they do indeed have what it takes to change their lives for the better.

Many people believe money will give them lasting power, but money often disap-points. It fails to provide inner strength. Money is an energy form that flows or doesn't flow, depending on your relationship with it. Money is essential, of course. We need it to meet our commitments and reach our goals. It also can provide great opportunities for joy and new experiences. But if you value yourself solely for the money you make, what does that mean when you lose your job, your livelihood, your income? Does that mean you are a powerless, worthless individual? Does it mean that until you find a new job or higher income you're not important or your life isn't essential? Defining your worth as a human being by your income or your cash value typically leads to feelings of powerlessness and inefficacy. You'll end up feeling more like a servant to money than a master of it.

Security, too, is elusive unless you are secure within yourself. A great salary, a terrific employer, wonderful benefits, a high-powered job, a spouse, a beautiful home . . . these things can't bring real security because they can be lost or taken away. Real security is knowing that you have all you need inside yourself to weather life's challenges.

So how can you count less on money and external objects to give you strength and more on your inner power? First, let's look at your beliefs about your ability to access your power.

Unleashing Your Power

1. In your opinion, how capable are you of tapping into the vast power you have inside you? Circle the number that best reflects your answer. (To help

you stay away from "5"—which leaves you on the fence—"X" appears in its place.)

Not at All Capable   Very Capable

| | | 1 | 2 | 3 | 4 | X | 6 | 7 | 8 | 9 | 10 |

2. If you circled "4" or less, who or what holds you back from unleashing your power?
3. What are you connected to *outside yourself* that keeps you feeling powerless (money, salary, job, another person, etc.)?
4. In what ways can you slowly take back your power from this outside entity and restore it in yourself?

_____

5. On a scale of 1 to 5 (1 = no access; 5 = direct access), what number reflects the degree to which you believe you have access to the following qualities in yourself?

	No Access				Direct Access
Courage	1	2	3	4	5
Self-esteem	1	2	3	4	5
Patience	1	2	3	4	5
Perseverance	1	2	3	4	5
Strength	1	2	3	4	5
Flexibility	1	2	3	4	5
Energy	1	2	3	4	5
Faith	1	2	3	4	5
Honesty	1	2	3	4	5
Self-love	1	2	3	4	5
Balance	1	2	3	4	5
Perspective	1	2	3	4	5
Inner security	1	2	3	4	5
Ability to ask for help	1	2	3	4	5

a. What one quality do you feel in greatest need of right now?

_____

b. What one step can you take today to help you develop this quality, to help you access your inner power?

_____

Disentangle from Your Struggle

As Marsha pointed out, reconnecting to your real self and accessing your inner power calls for finding ways to disengage from your current struggle. When you separate yourself from what you're enmeshed in, new insights and alternatives come to light. Taking time out from your struggle can illuminate repeated negative patterns that need to be reversed.

When I took time out after being laid off, I was amazed at the world around me—so many different professions, businesses, and creative work opportunities that I had never seen or focused on before. Stepping off the hamster wheel allowed me to take in the many diverse ways people purposefully choose to live their lives and contribute meaningfully to the world. I also saw my power struggles differently. Several years before, my accountant had said to my husband, "Wow, she's a keeper!" referring to how much money I contributed to our household. After being laid off, I became aware that for many years I too had valued myself as a "keeper" because of my income. When the money went away, I wondered, "Am I still 'a keeper'?" Thank goodness, both my husband and I now know that the answer is "Yes!"

How can you take time out from your power struggles? It's critical to find new ways to disengage—for an hour, day, week, or however long you can—from what disempowers you, and dedicate time to restoring your awareness of your inner power and worth.

MOVING FORWARD TO BREAKTHROUGH

✳ STEP BACK

Let's start by helping you explore where falseness exists in your life. Think about work, home, friends, family, and the roles you play in life. Where do you feel you can be "true" to yourself, and where can't you be? Check one column for each.

Roles You Play	Feeling True?	Feeling False?
Professional Life		
Employee		
Boss		
Manager		
Colleague		
Team member		
Leader		
Mentor		
Assistant		
Other		
Personal Life		
Parent		
Spouse		
Sibling		
Child		
Family member		
Friend		
Other		

For all the roles in which you feel you're being false in some way, how are you false? In what ways are you not saying, being, and doing what is right for you? Write down all the ways you're not being true to yourself.

_____

_____

_____

What steps can you take to be more true to yourself in these roles?

1. Role: _____

What I can do to be true to myself:

_____

2. Role: _____

What I can do to be true to myself:

_____

3. Role: _____

What I can do to be true to myself:

_____

4. Role: _____

What I can do to be true to myself:

_____

Commit to taking these actions starting today.

✳ **LET GO** of giving up your power to others or things.

Think about the situation that is causing you the most distress at this time. In your journal, capture all your thoughts. *No censoring, please—write everything that comes to mind.*

- What have you empowered over yourself (money, security, prestige, accomplishments, other people, etc.)?
- What are all the reasons that you've done so (childhood experiences, recent events, challenges, traumas)?
- If these outer things (money, etc.) were to go away today, how would you see yourself? How would you describe yourself to others?
- Without these outer trappings, what makes you special, unique, important, worthy?
- How are you a "keeper" because of who you are inside?

- What life lessons have you learned that make you a powerful force of good in the world?
- How ready are you to stop giving up your power to this outside entity?
- How will you begin to empower yourself today?

✳ **SAY YES!** to acting in alignment with the *real* you.

Recommended Steps

1. Understand where you are being false to yourself. Quietly go inward and ask yourself—consult your inner guidance, your intuition—to tell you:

   - Where am I being false to myself, speaking or being less than honest and authentic?
   - What words would be more true for me right now?
   - To whom do I need to say these words?
   - What actions are false for me?
   - What actions would be more authentic?

   Take out your journal, and write down what your intuitive voice and heart have shared. Review the information. Allow it to soak in.

2. Ask yourself, "What one step can I take this month to bring forward authentic and true actions and words, rather than suppress them?" Write down the answer, and commit to taking this one small step this month.

Remember

Learn to love and accept yourself as you are, flaws and all. You need to discover and connect with the *real* you every day, and honor that in every word, thought, and action.

Marsha reminds us

"Right after 9/11, my little son looked outside and said, 'Look, Mom, there are still birds and trees.' I thought to myself, 'Life is so simple and good, but we make it so challenging.' I'm dedicated now to giving up the struggle, and living every day as honestly and openly as I can. I'm doing my best, and accepting with love and patience all that I am."

✳ **BREAKTHROUGH** "I love and accept myself."

EMPOWERMENT WITH OTHERS

7

Speaking Up
with Power

A No uttered from deepest conviction
is better and greater than a Yes
merely uttered to please or,
what is worse, to avoid trouble.

MAHATMA GANDHI

✳ **STEP BACK TO EXPLORE** Reliving past trauma over speaking up.

✳ **LET GO** of your pain from past suppression.

✳ **SAY YES!** to your personal power through words and action.

✳ **BREAKTHROUGH**

"I use my voice to support myself and others."

✳ **Christine:** *I have a long history of not being able to speak up for myself. I see now that how I was raised and what I went through growing up stunted my ability to know myself. I couldn't express what I believed or wanted. And often, I didn't even know what I thought deep down. My very traditional, conservative parents came from cultures that believed women and children should be seen and not heard, so that's how I was trained. Throughout my life, I can't ever remember asking myself, "What do I really want to say here?" because it didn't seem like a relevant question. My thoughts and feelings weren't allowed to come to the surface.*

I learned early on that if I spoke up to my father or challenged him, he would either become enraged or shut down and completely withdraw for hours, sometimes days. This repeated experience of being rejected left me believing that speaking up for myself, even if done with respect and care, would have dire consequences. My mother didn't stand up for me, either, so I felt completely alone. After experiencing this rejection over and over, I just stopped expressing my real thoughts or feelings to Dad or anyone else, especially if they were contradictory or challenging in any way. As the years went on, I was forced to speak up more in my jobs, but I still couldn't do it well or easily. This inability to speak up for myself, or to identify my true beliefs and needs, became chronic. From as early as I can remember until about a year ago, I rarely followed my heart or stood up for what I believed. I'd make attempts, but they always came out tentative and unsure, or insecure, angry, and defensive. I pursued experiences, relationships, and jobs that I thought others (mostly my parents) would approve of. I know I was very negative and critical about myself (and others), too, mostly because I felt so unhappy and because others seemed to be doing so much better than I was.

✳ Christine (not her real name) is a 46-year-old director of a consumer products firm.

A while ago, in my job as director for a small consumer products firm, I experienced a series of serious setbacks. I was having conflicts with several peers in other departments, as well as difficult challenges with one important client and one department head in particular. I tried to speak up authoritatively in ways that would bring about productive change, but each time I did, something worse seemed to happen. My coworkers saw me as a bully, as someone who gets things done but leaves a wake of angry people behind. The more I spoke up, the more others became defensive and critical and seemed to wanted to drum me out. I had one staunch supporter in the senior ranks, but the rest seemed hell-bent to crush me. Then my work situation became intolerable—I experienced discrimination, harassment, insults, and ridicule, and eventually I was put on probation for reasons that weren't at all about performance. I finally got mad, really mad, and snapped. I decided enough was enough. I wasn't going to keep quiet any longer.

Christine's story reveals her longtime inability to speak up effectively on her own behalf. When she did speak up, her words came across as bullying and overly aggressive, masking her fear of standing up for herself. This fear emerged from her prolonged conditioning that there would be serious negative consequences if she did. As children, when we're rejected for being ourselves, we resort to protecting ourselves and adhering to the status quo to remain safe, accepted, and loved. Many women have experienced this type of suppression in childhood, which reinforces a deep lack of self-trust and self-advocacy. Parents do the best they can, of course, but many were (and are) taught that good parenting is about telling children what to do and think at every turn. Wrong. Often, parents can't tolerate being challenged because their own self-esteem is fragile. Being challenged means that they're being rejected by their children. To insecure individuals, this rejection equates with being unloved or disrespected.

The most critical traits to foster in a child are unwavering self-love, self-reliance, and self-respect. Teaching your child to trust herself, and to speak up and out on her own behalf (even if it means she's going to challenge you as the parent), is the best gift you can give. Also critical is teaching effective and positive communication skills. Learning how to articulate your needs and wants so that others will meet you halfway is as important as speaking up.

As the renowned humanist psychologist Carl Rogers explained,[1] when we are allowed to follow our own inner guidance as our highest authority, and express what's important to us, we thrive and achieve for ourselves positive forward movement. Those who can do this lead fuller, happier, healthier, and more empowered lives. But developing these capabilities, of following your own inner guidance and speaking up for yourself with confidence, courage, and centeredness when you need to, is extremely difficult—especially when you felt unsafe, unloved, or shut down each time you stood up for yourself as a child.

Standing Up for Yourself

Many women experience fear and worry over speaking up for themselves. Often they think they'll feel even more vulnerable or powerless by articulating what they want or need. They ask me, "Why should I have to say what I want or need? Isn't it obvious? Why do I have to go through this?" My answer is that in order for you to gain the courage you need to direct your life with satisfaction and not feel like a powerless victim, you have to speak up for what's true for you, no matter how frightening, angering, or diminishing it feels.

If you've felt suppressed ever since childhood, you might wonder, "What can I do about that now? It's done." I believe you can overcome this experience and heal by taking courageous action today—using positive language that supports and reaffirms who you are and what you think and believe. A powerful little book, *The Four Agreements*, by Don Miguel Ruiz, discusses the immense impact of being "impeccable with your word."[2] In this guide, Ruiz talks about the power words have in the world, the importance of using your words in ways that don't bring harm, criticism, negativity, or diminishment, or "sin" against yourself and others.

Using your words powerfully and positively requires that you always *speak the truth*. This doesn't mean you will be cruel or say hurtful things. This means you will state, with as much love, care, and compassion as you can, what the truth is for you. Using "I" statements about how you are feeling and perceiving others' actions and outside events can be helpful. When you feel upset or put down, or if your boundaries are being violated, you need to speak up, not with blaming language but with "I" statements that reflect your view without making someone else wrong. "I" statements express what you're feeling yet leave room for others to hear what you're saying and openly express their thoughts and feelings.

Here are some examples of "I" statements:

To a spouse: "When you cut me off in mid-sentence, I feel frustrated because I'm not able to say what I want to and I don't feel heard."

To a friend: "I'm disappointed when you put other things ahead of getting together with me because I feel I'm unimportant to you."

To an employee: "I value promptness at my meetings because to me being on time reflects respect for others and commitment to the work. Please come on time."

To a business partner: "I'd like there to be mutual respect between us. When you call me at all hours of the night, I get frustrated because I feel my private time with my family is not being respected."

"I" statements help you assert what's true for you without creating the need for others to protect and defend themselves. Try it out. Speak up for yourself, starting today. Don't wait. You'll be amazed at the results. Figure out what you need to say that you've been keeping inside. How have your boundaries been invaded, and with whom do you need to discuss that? Have you been treated disrespectfully? What do you need to say in your life and work that you're not communicating? Find a way to speak up now.

Christine explains: *When I snapped, I decided that this had to stop. I realized I needed help, so I got it. I went to a professional coach and pursued legal counsel, all of which helped me see that I had indeed been on the receiving end of professional behavior that was unacceptable and unethical, but that I had, in part, acted insufficiently and unproductively on my own behalf for a long time. My lack of trusting myself or being able to communicate in professional, authoritative, and confident ways about the real problems at work led me away from getting the results I wanted. I'd either overreact and get very emotional or withdraw defensively, just as my father had. I stayed stuck far too long, when I should have believed in myself and spoken up in more direct, productive ways to the leaders and decision-makers who could really make a difference, rather than complain behind people's backs.*

With outside help, I found a way to advocate for myself, and I told the powers that be, in a series of long and hard meetings, what I wanted to see changed and what I deserved. Drawing on support from the outside, I got some wind in my sails and felt stronger in my words and convictions. I realized finally (and was able to express myself so they listened) the importance and huge financial benefit of my past contributions to the company. By getting an outside and informed perspective, I learned that what I wanted was not outlandish but reasonable, well-deserved, and appropriate. In fact, the changes I suggested for myself and the company were clearly good for the organization's long-term health.

Christine says of her life now: *Unbelievably, standing up for myself in this fashion shifted everything for me. I got what I asked for, and the discrimination was also handled effectively by the company. For once in my life, I felt that speaking up for myself was the right* *thing to do—a powerful and helpful thing for myself, for others, and for the company. A year later, I can say that I'm a better and more successful manager, leader, and employee, because I feel more respect for myself and my thinking, actions, and contributions. It's still not easy to speak up, but I don't hesitate as much. I try to say what needs to be said as soon as it's appropriate. I still get outside help when I need it, but that's okay. I'm on the road to feeling good about trusting who I am and what I believe, and acting on that. I like the work I do so much more now, and I'm happy I found a way to make it work for me. I've recently received really positive feedback and a strong performance review as well, which I feel great about.*

CHRISTINE'S ADVICE

- Ask yourself all the time, every day, "What do I want to say here?" and move toward expressing that, without being overly emotional or reactive. Learn to trust yourself and communicate what's important and relevant to you, even though you're not used to accepting that as valid.
- Find ways to express yourself and what you want without putting yourself or others down. Avoid talking behind people's backs, and avoid language that reflects blame, accusations, negativity, criticism, or insecurity.
- Get outside help to give you an informed, fresh perspective about what you want and what is appropriate for you. Take the time to look at how you were suppressed in the past. You can overcome the frustration, fear, and hopelessness you experienced by asserting yourself as you go forward.

Say What You Want to Say

Speaking the truth sounds simple, but it's not. We're often unsure how to do it because we're afraid we'll make others mad or hurt people's feelings, or we'll be rejected or lose control of our tempers if we tell it like it is. The obvious corollary to speaking the truth is *avoiding lies.* Lying—making untrue statements with the intent to deceive or create a false or misleading impression—and its ramifications have been the subject of many conversations I've had with clients. Over and over, clients have admitted that lies they've told or basic truths they've denied have led them on long detours away from what they now feel is their "right" path. These detours happened because they based their actions on falsehoods rather than truth or authenticity. The most essential reason lying is destructive is that it robs you and others of being able to evaluate accurately and fully how best to move forward.

When you lie to others, you limit their ability to make the right choices and decisions for themselves. And when you can't state outwardly what you know is true inwardly, you prevent your own life from moving forward in a healthy and positive way. Instead, you take wrong steps based on half-truths or inconsistencies, which inevitably lead you to living a half-life and half-experiences. The bottom line: Lying keeps you stuck.

Being in denial keeps you stuck as well. I define denial as either a refusal to accept what you believe is true, or a refusal to acknowledge painful realities, thoughts, or feelings. Denial as a coping mechanism can be helpful for survival, but if chronic it can keep you from moving forward in ways that are important to your growth. In refusing to accept what isn't working, you enforce your internal belief that you are too weak, frightened, flawed, or incompetent to deal with or act on the truth. Denial can also emerge when you're afraid of living your full potential, of shining your light too brightly. Many brilliant, skilled, and accomplished—in a word, *powerful*—people deny their gifts and their potentially large sphere of influence because they buy into the fear that they simply aren't good enough (the old "impostor" syndrome we know so well). "Who am I to believe I can follow my dream and make it happen?" they ask themselves, habitually denying their creative power. Sometimes we walk away from our own power and brilliance because leaving the "tribe" behind is a daunting endeavor.

Someone once said, "Greater awareness equals greater choice." This statement reminds us that when you allow yourself to remain unaware or unaccepting of your true thoughts, feelings, motives, and so on, life will certainly unfold *as it will*, but you won't be charting its course. Instead, the flight plan used to guide your life will be out of your view. And when you lie, you steal from your mind, body, and spirit the opportunity of fully experiencing yourself—of bringing about the natural consequences of your authentic thoughts, words, and deeds. Lying is the ultimate act of manipulation by a threatened ego.

Typical Lies and Denials

People tend to lie about or deny in themselves emotions or experiences that make them feel vulnerable, afraid, or small, such as:

- Actions they've taken that they're ashamed of
- Feelings of deep loss, sadness, hurt, and frustration
- Dissatisfaction with their current situations
- The sense of being overwhelmed and exhausted
- Fears that they are failing or letting others down
- Problems and past mistakes that still haunt them
- Feelings of isolation
- Yearnings that "there must be more to life than this"

New Truths

When you do the work of getting in touch with what you want to express in yourself, and articulating it, life changes. You become stronger, more confident, more stable, and more able to direct your life and work as you desire. You also become aware of various truths that previously were not clear. You'll understand that:

- You are co-creating much of what you experience.
- You *do* have what it takes to change the direction of your life for the better.
- You are whole, powerful, and creative, despite the problems and challenges you have experienced.
- You are worthy of having your dreams come true.
- You are lovable and acceptable.
- You have an essential purpose in the world.
- To live this essential purpose, you must speak up.
- You have access to the strength and help you need to speak up for yourself.
- There *is* more to life than what you're experiencing now.

Learning to speak up for yourself takes courage, effort, patience, perseverance, and practice, if you're not used to doing it. A few guidelines to speaking up for yourself effectively and powerfully will help you progress on that path:

- Have certainty behind your words, because you know that they are true for you.
- Be open to how others interpret your words, and learn from their input and views.
- Avoid blaming or criticizing others in your language.
- Avoid speaking ill of others and yourself.

- Take accountability for all your words and actions.
- Don't shy away from what you have to say, but remember to say it with love, compassion, and centeredness.
- If you can't say it with compassion, get help to gain a new perspective that allows for reduced emotionality and pain.
- How people respond is more about them than you.

Telling your own truth is one of the most powerful keys to unlocking and bringing into being creative power. No matter how well-intended, lying or keeping quiet limits you because it forces essential aspects of you to go underground. Remember, your words are extremely powerful—like weapons if used hatefully, or like beacons of light, if used with confidence, love, and truth.

Use Positive Language

I've seen in my own life how destructive negative words can be. Harsh criticisms have stayed with me a lifetime, whereas I have easily forgotten loving words. I've made it an absolute rule to avoid as much as possible using critical, judgmental, or harsh words about myself and others. If I slip up and let something ugly fly out of my mouth, I try to revise it, right then and there. I stop and say to myself, "I'd like to delete that, and say _____ instead." I then replace the sharp words with something more accepting and open, something that allows in possibility rather than negativity. This process has been transformational. Gaining awareness of how you are critical of others helps you stop being that way to yourself. Gossiping and speaking ill about others is a habit that causes suffering, your own and others'.

Starting today, observe your language. Are your words and phrases mostly positive, hopeful, and encouraging? Or are they critical, disparaging, disapproving, fault-finding, and unsympathetic? How you speak of and view others directly mirrors how you view yourself. So what does your language about other people say about how you esteem yourself? If you accuse and blame others frequently, stop now. If you put yourself down, stop now. Make it a habit to choose language that reflects acceptance, hope, kindness, compassion, and forgiveness. You will be amazed at the shifts that become possible within you when you foster positive language rather than feed negativity. It's simple: Let your language speak of your power, goodness, and strength, not of your weaknesses and flaws.

Heal Past Suppression

As Christine did, sometimes we all need a fresh perspective to help us see where we are not loving or honoring ourselves as well as we could. An outside, neutral yet expansive view of who you are, what you deserve in life, and the tremendous power you hold can be instrumental and assist you in uncovering how your past has suppressed you. Whether it's a psychotherapist, a coach, or a friend who believes wholeheartedly in you, the form of help is less important than your receiving it. Others can help you step out of your limited view and gain a new perspective that reframes your past experiences for the better.

If your past is all about how you couldn't speak up, now is the time to revise the lessons you learned. Make your past about what you've overcome, what you've risen above, and how strong it has made you. Your present can now be about your integrity, truthfulness, and compassion, your strength and courage, and your willingness to express what is true for you and be supportive of others. Choosing to look at your past this way makes room for seeing that many of the reasons you couldn't speak up are no longer valid. They no longer exist.

Being an effective and authentic communicator helps others feel safe, secure, and accepted in your presence as well. Your presence allows them to be real, true, and authentic in their lives and work.

MOVING FORWARD TO BREAKTHROUGH

✷ STEP BACK

What does your language say about you? Observe your words closely this week.

- How would you and others describe the words and phrases you use? Are they kind, sympathetic, encouraging, and optimistic? Or are they judgmental, unforgiving, severe, or intolerant?
- What does your spoken language say about you? What does it say about your view of others?
- Are you able to speak up effectively so people can hear you without becoming defensive?

- What does your physical (body) language say about you? (Confident, shy, afraid, powerful, welcoming, etc.)
- What do you *want* your words and language to reveal about you?
- Find a role model—someone who speaks confidently, truthfully, yet compassionately. Observe the words s/he uses.
- Revise your negative language to be positive.

  The negative phrase I use most often is _____.

  I will replace that phrase with _____.

✳ LET GO of your pain from past suppression.

Think about the situation that is causing you the most distress at this time. In your journal, capture all your thoughts. *No censoring, please—write everything that comes to mind.*

- How were you suppressed in your expression of who you are (your thoughts, words, beliefs, actions, values, etc.) in your childhood or early life?
- Who suppressed you the most?
- What might have been the reasons that this person didn't allow you full expression? Was s/he somehow intimidated by you, your power, spontaneity, beauty, sexuality, joyfulness, creativity? Was s/he afraid of being rejected by you?
- How has this suppression affected you?
- How does it affect you today?
- How has it made you stronger?
- If this suppression hadn't occurred, how would your life be different today?
- How ready are you to let go of the pain of your past suppression?

  Very   Somewhat   Not at All

- What help can you receive to heal this suppression and move forward?

✳ **SAY YES!** to your personal power through words and action.

Recommended Steps

1. Quietly go inward and ask yourself—consult your inner guidance, your intuition—to explore the following:

   - Sit quietly and think about: "How am I not telling the whole truth to myself or another person now?"
   - Now turn it over in your mind. What *is* the full truth for me?
   - What does this truth mean in my life, exactly?
   - What has kept me from telling the truth? (Hurting feelings, being rejected, facing difficult consequences, upsetting the peace, etc.)
   - Now ask yourself, "What must I say now, and to whom, to move forward on my path?"
   - Can I say what I must, calmly but with conviction?
   - What help can I get this month to say what I need to say, effectively?

   Take out your journal, and write down what your intuitive voice and heart have shared. Review the information. Allow it to soak in.

2. Commit to taking one small step this week to telling an essential truth that needs to be told.

Remember

You are here to support and assert the positive, powerful person you are. Suppression is a lesson from your life that is waiting to be healed and overcome.

Christine reminds us

"It's not easy to speak up for yourself with honesty and self-confidence. But it can change everything for the better when you do. Don't be afraid to get outside help if you need to, and remember that you have a right to your thoughts and feelings, and expressing them to others is your right as well."

✳ **BREAKTHROUGH** "I use my voice to support myself and others."

8

Breaking Cycles
of Mistreatment

As long as you think that the cause of your problem
is "out there"—as long as you think that anyone
or anything is responsible for your suffering—
the situation is hopeless. It means that you are forever
in the role of victim, that you're suffering in paradise.

BYRON KATIE
Loving What Is

EMPOWERMENT WITH OTHERS

❋ **Anne:** *My life has been a full and extraordinary one, with many blessings, including my four children and eight beloved grandchildren. But I've had a fair share of adversity, too. My father adored me, but he was an abusive man—physically, verbally, and emotionally—and he was particularly cruel to my mother. She resented me terribly because I was spared most of his abuse, and because he loved me. Mother was full of rage and jealousy and treated me like a hostile invader. My father had a violent temper, abused my mother physically, neglected her emotional needs, and cheated on and deceived her, yet she stayed and endured his treatment for sixty-five years.*

As a young adult, I went to college and then moved to New York, where I got a job in retail. My goal was to earn enough money to get an apartment and to find a man to marry. I soon met "Mr. Right" and thought I was in love with him, until we were on our honeymoon, and he became violent and abusive. I knew right then, down to my bones, that staying with him would lead to suffering. I confronted him with my decision to leave him, but I allowed him to dissuade me by talking about the guilt I would feel after my parents had given me such a lovely wedding, what would they tell their friends, etc. And he promised that his abusive behavior would never happen again. So I didn't leave, and the cycle of abuse started then.

For twenty-five years, I stayed with my husband, through his furies, his alcoholism, his mistreatment, his recurrent lost jobs, and his failure to provide for us. We had periods of happiness, but they were interspersed with regular bouts of physical and emotional abuse, suffering, fear, secrecy, and terrible sadness.

Then I was diagnosed with breast cancer. At the same time a therapist's question proved catalytic when he asked, "How can you expect people to respect you when you don't respect yourself?" Suddenly I was shocked with the realization that I didn't have to accept this

❋ Anne is a 69-year-old small-business owner. 95

abusive behavior. These two events were the beginning of a tremendous shift for me, when I knew, finally, that I had to leave my husband and find a way to make it on my own, or I wouldn't survive. I began to piece together a plan to leave, and I decided I had to find a way to earn money for myself so I could be self-reliant and free.

Sadly, Anne's story is not uncommon, and tells the universal tale of women who have experienced physical violence and emotional abuse as a child, only to relive them again as they build their own families. Anne's primary role model as a woman and a wife was her mother, someone desperate for love and attention who, in her neediness and insecurity, accepted this type of pain and suffering. Anne's mother even encouraged her daughter to remain in her abusive marriage, because this had been her "fate."

Due to Anne's troubled childhood, she developed a profound longing for love and acceptance and would do almost anything to receive it. As is often the case for individuals who are abused in childhood, her boundaries—the invisible barriers that surround you as an individual and regulate the input from and output to the outside world—were damaged and overly diffuse, leaving her vulnerable to abusive behavior. Until her life-threatening illness, she remained frozen in her marital situation, unable to move forward in an empowered way to either protect or remove herself and her children from it.

Cycles of abuse are complicated, intricate, and interwoven, often passed down from generations, and not easily broken. But these cycles can be overcome, as thousands of women can attest. Anne broke free as well, only to discover more about her inner strengths—and her vulnerabilities.

Anne Breaks Free

I decided to take action. After attending a focus group as a participant at a market research firm nearby, I was intrigued by the process and thought that running focus groups was a skill I could develop without having to get further education. So I got my foot in the door by offering my services as an assistant. From that point on, I focused on learning the trade, soaking up everything I saw and heard. I soon began to moderate focus groups myself and was quite good at it. Clients began to request me for projects. I gained a solid understanding of what was involved in running a successful small research firm. I worked there for about ten years, established a name for myself in the field, then decided to start my own business.

My business began to make a nice profit, and I became financially secure for the first time. Within the first year, I made enough money to support myself, and I bought a condo in Florida—ostensibly as a vacation home, but secretly I knew it was my escape route, my safe haven. After two years of working in my own firm, I moved out of the house where my husband lived and moved into my new Florida home. I'll never forget walking into my condo near the white sand beach I so loved, locking the door behind me, and leaning against it weeping, repeating over and over, "I'm safe, I'm safe, I'm safe."

Anne found within herself new resolve, and deeper courage and conviction to take bold action to free herself from a life of abuse and suffering. The universe often conspires to help us when we stand up for ourselves and commit to moving forward in honoring ourselves. Carving out a new professional niche, she embraced it with every ounce of energy and commitment she could muster. She succeeded and forged new life possibilities. But she soon discovered that mistreatment wasn't completely gone from her life. It surfaced again, in other forms.

I worked very hard building my business and was open to taking any client that came my way. I had large financial goals for myself and was committed to achieving them. I was great at my work, and offered superior service, and many clients gave me repeat business. But soon enough, something happened that gave me pause. Clients began to creep in who treated me poorly, took advantage of me, or made me the scapegoat. I remember one situation in which a new client failed to prepare me sufficiently for a research project I was hired to execute. After I had delivered the first focus group of many that were booked, they came in and fired me on the spot, yelling that I simply didn't know what I was doing, even though the account exec at the agency had failed to provide me with the appropriate background info. I experienced other forms of mistreatment, too, from clients who publicly ridiculed me to those who tried to influence me about research results. I've been cheated, back-stabbed, fired for unjust cause, and harassed through the years. Again, I tolerated this type of treatment, kept coming back for more, trying to determine how I'd blown it and how I could win these clients back.

As Anne describes, mistreatment in her business became a more-than-occasional occurrence. How many women do you know who have been severely mistreated in their professional lives? I've personally experienced numerous forms of mistreatment at work over the years, from both men and women, including harassment, discrimination, being passed over for promotion by a colleague with ten years' less experience, being treated punitively for speaking up . . . the list goes on. Controversial as this may sound, I believe that our male colleagues do not suffer in the same way from these types of infringements. Why?

The answer is of course complex and many-fold, but I believe part of it lies in women's relative lack of an internal, unfaltering sense of strength, power, and confidence. In our society, women are relatively new to the ranks of power and authority and are still finding their legs. Further, women in general are more motivated by interpersonal connection and mutuality. They're influenced heavily by how others perceive them, and they typically invest more time and energy in evaluating the degree to which they are accepted, approved of, and respected. Women's interest in how others relate to them makes them more vulnerable to acting in ways designed to win acceptance.

Although I was not subjected to physical or verbal abuse in my childhood, as was Anne, I developed overly diffuse boundaries that kept me longing for acceptance. I did not recognize mistreatment, nor did I take timely, proactive measures to remove myself from it. Now recognizing my own weak boundaries, I realize that from the beginning of my professional journey to the end of my corporate career, I gave pieces of myself away, big pieces, in order to be accepted and liked.

Thankfully, like Anne, I no longer desperately need anyone's approval or acceptance. I've worked hard to develop stronger boundaries that allow me to remain firm in my own convictions and to take action to support them despite the realization that such action may rock the boat. I can now recognize immediately when I'm on the receiving end of behavior that feels vengeful, unethical, abusive, narcissistic, or downright wrong. Being able to move away from mistreatment and abuse once and for all requires several key developments: growing in your self-acceptance and self-love, increasing your connection to your own values and convictions, gaining greater awareness of the signs of mistreatment, developing the courage to speak up about your limits, and taking action to remove or protect yourself from ill-treatment the moment you see it.

Anne's Journey to Empowerment

Then I had a catastrophic blow, a life-changing experience. In 1990, I met the man of my dreams, and we quickly entered into a wonderful, passionate relationship that seemed the answer to my lifelong prayers. In my mind, he was the ardent lover and intimate partner I'd never had but so desired. We were together several months, and all of a sudden, I couldn't believe it, yet there they were again—signs of an abusive, rageful manipulator, a Svengali of sorts. But I ignored these signs, I couldn't accept them, mainly because this was the man who gave me passionate love and completed me. We loved each other deeply and planned to marry, despite the clues I received that he might become abusive over time. I never found out what our relationship would grow to be. He died of a massive heart attack in my arms, just weeks before we were to be married.

This loss was the most heartbreaking, excruciating experience I've ever been through. For a year, I could barely function. Only my work and my children kept me alive. But after a year passed, something began to shift, and I began to grow a bit stronger, and heal. I vowed then never to relinquish that much of myself again to anyone or anything. I suddenly saw how, all my life, my insatiable need to be loved, accepted, and cherished had kept me frightened and insecure, and had perpetuated my feelings of unworthiness and inferiority. My neediness blocked me from identifying mistreatment and from walking away from it. So I decided it had to stop. I sought help from many different sources. I received therapy, joined a powerful women's support group, and connected to a new sense of spirituality, on my terms. I also built a network of wonderfully strong and inspiring women friends, from whom I continually receive support, guidance, and love when I need it most.

Anne says of her life now: *It's been seventeen years since I lost the love of my life, and I've learned a great deal about myself since then. I've done so much work to strengthen myself, develop healthier boundaries, wake up to my own needs, and stop placing everyone else first. I've had breast cancer a second time and gone through a double mastectomy and reconstruction. But I'm tougher now, more aware and conscious, attempting every day to love and honor myself in ways I couldn't have dreamt of before. I'm a survivor.*

My business still sustains my financial and professional needs, but I do things on my terms now. I've surpassed my financial goals, and I take only the clients I feel comfortable with—those who will be stimulating to work with and respectful to me. I'm clearer about my boundaries, and about who I will let into my life, and how I will allow them to treat me. I see how my lack of self-love and my fear of rejection kept me victimized, and I've stepped out of that for good now.

I'm a Guardian Ad Litem for the state now, and I advocate for the safety of abused, abandoned, and neglected children. It's very fulfilling. I feel like I'm righting many of the wrongs that occurred in my childhood. I've also found tremendous fulfillment and spiritual growth being with several friends in the end stages of their lives. As I've lived through serious illness and faced the real possibility of my own death, I can be empathetic and understand the emotional needs of those with terminal illnesses. I have helped people live with greater love and acceptance, courage, openness, and deeper connection with their families. My life is rich and full now, and I know that I am loved and respected by others and, more importantly, by myself. My hardships have made me who I am, and I'm grateful for my life.

Anne's story teaches us about the long-term effects of abuse, the intense courage required to strengthen ourselves and gain self-efficacy, and about what life unexpectedly delivers to push us along a path of empowerment and growth. Certainly we're shaped by what we're born with and given in childhood, but that beginning isn't nearly the end of the story. We have our entire lives to grow, learn, stretch, get reconnected to who we are at our core, and forge a more joyful and satisfying way to live and work.

ANNE'S ADVICE

- Develop healthy, strong boundaries, and see clearly where you end and others begin. Be clear about what you will allow and what you won't, and protect these limits.
- Stop pleasing others to address your own neediness. Look at how you live your life—if it's all about catering to the needs and wishes of others, stop and rethink why you give so much of yourself away every day.
- Get help and advocacy to step out of the cycle of abuse. Find a trusted organization, support group, therapist, or friend who can advocate for you and provide you with a fresh perspective about what you're enduring. See your world through these neutral eyes, and listen when your advocates tell you that you don't have to live this way any longer.

Develop Strong Boundaries

Boundaries are the invisible barriers that separate you from the world around you. They define who you are, and they keep you safe and secure, physically, emotionally, and spiritually. Having well-developed boundaries ensures that you are shielded from behaviors and actions that are injurious, disrespectful, or invasive. Those with healthy boundaries know their limits and are able to express them with quiet strength and authority. Healthy boundaries—well-established limits as to what you expect and need from others and what you will and will not tolerate in others' actions and words—allow you to move forward on a fulfilling and satisfying path. Of course, you can't control other people's actions and words, but you can control your response to them, as well as your actions in the face of language and behavior that violate who you have defined yourself to be in this world.

If your boundaries are weak, others can disturb you, invade your privacy, suck your energy, drain your resources . . . in short, behave parasitically, taking from you whatever you allow them to.

Healthy, strong boundaries ensure that you:

- Experience and demonstrate self-respect and respect of others
- Understand and articulate effectively the limits you've set for yourself
- Know unequivocally when your limits have been overstepped
- Determine with sureness the actions you wish to take when your boundaries have been invaded
- Live well with the consequences of enforcing your boundaries

A few basic steps are required to strengthen your boundaries, and none of them are easily done. Boundary development requires courage, patience, and time, but it is well worth the investment, and life-changing when achieved.

First, it's important to gain awareness of what you need more of in your life and work. What do you desperately long for—more time, energy, honesty, compassion, respect, care, commitment, or power? Begin the process of exploring when you feel thwarted, angry, resentful, drained, and undervalued. Most likely your boundaries could use bolstering in these situations. Once you recognize what you need, set clear and unwavering limits as to what you desire and need from others to feel respected and valued. Think about it, write it down—what are your rules going forward in terms of what you expect, need, and will allow from others?

Then communicate these limits to the outside world calmly, clearly, and unemotionally. Know in your heart and mind what the consequences will be if people don't respect your limits. What will you do? Will you speak to them, asking them again to respect your wishes? Will you walk away? If, after several attempts to communicate what you need, they still won't respect your limits, will you end your association, or limit it? In addition, you must ask yourself, "How will I respect the boundaries of others? What new actions must I take to treat others the way I'm defining as essential for myself? When am I not respecting others' boundaries?"

I remember a few years ago deciding to walk away from the habit of gossiping or speaking negatively of others. I had done it all my life, triangulated to ease my own anxiety, and spoken critically about one friend or family member to the other. I realized that this was a destructive habit fed by my own insecurities, and I knew it always came back to hurt me. But since I'd been doing it for years, I needed to communicate to the people I knew that I no longer wanted to engage in this type of behavior. The next time a friend spoke ill of another in front of me, I said, "I know I used to in the past, but I'm working really hard on not speaking ill of others, or gossiping, so I'm not comfortable with this conversation. Would you mind if we changed the subject?" I was shocked to see the result. People not only obliged my request, but also seemed to respect me more. I've spoken up now about my limits regarding many aspects of my life, and I'm still truly amazed at the power that comes from communicating and enforcing your limits. These boundaries allow you to design and live the life you dream of, because they reflect how you respect and honor yourself. Maintaining your limits in turn paves the way for others to treat you with the same esteem.

Stop Pleasing Others to Fill Your Needs

Anne learned she was pleasing others to fulfill her own neediness. Accommodation can be healthy and caring. But often for women, it is a self-demeaning act, showing that we place more importance on others' needs and desires than on our own. Why do we overly accommodate and acquiesce to another's wishes when they do not match our own? The key reason is fear. We're afraid that love and approval will be withheld if we are our authentic selves, afraid that others will become angry and reject us for being honest. We fear that we are not worthy enough, smart enough, or right enough to articulate that we don't agree with what is going on. We fear that if we stop giving in to the needs of others, they'll stop needing us, and we'll cease to matter.

Many women learned this acquiescence from their parents or adopted this behavior to survive their childhoods. Thousands were raised in homes that did not allow expression of true thoughts and feelings. Punishment, sometimes severe, often ensued when women asserted themselves and enforced their personal limits. But if you don't address your habitual pattern of accommodation to others now, this pattern will remain for a lifetime, forever tripping you up on your way to a happier, more fulfilling work and family life.

Get Help to Break the Cycle of Abuse

When mistreatment is occurring, women need outside support to facilitate their ability to recognize what's really happening, explore what needs to be changed, and get help to take safe, appropriate action. If you are experiencing abuse of any kind, help is available. Reach out to get the help you need. Please see the resources at the back of this book for a list of organizations and agencies that offer support to victims of abuse and violence.

In the workplace, if you're experiencing mistreatment, stop in your tracks, and make an evaluation of what's transpiring. Also look at how you may be contributing to or allowing the situation. If any of the statements below are true for you, then proactive, empowered action is called for.

- I'm being harassed and made to do things that feel wrong.
- I'm being passed over because I'm a woman.
- I'm being back-stabbed and maligned.
- I'm not allowed to say "no" to projects and assignments I don't want.
- I've been promised things by my supervisors that I'm not getting.
- My work is being sabotaged.
- Money is being withheld from me for no reason.
- I'm being punished or blamed for things I didn't do.
- I've been forced into a position that I don't want.
- I'm being excluded from meetings and other informational sources and networks that are essential for me to succeed at my job.
- My reviews have been good, but I'm not being rewarded as promised.
- I've been asked to do unethical/illegal things for the job/company.
- I have to work around the clock to get my job done, and I don't want to.

You get the idea. If any of the above are happening, mistreatment possibly is occurring, and proactive measures are needed. But first, try to get in closer touch with who you are, with what you will and will not accept, and know with sureness what you value in life and work, and what your limits are. Before you can act, gaining awareness specifically of what feels wrong and right to you is essential. Become very clear now—evaluate in detail anything that feels like a violation, and why. Get to know more intimately what you want in your personal and professional life, and identify what you will stand for, and what you will not, going forward.

The next critical step is to understand the role you may be playing in your mistreatment. Have you not communicated your discomfort or your lack of agreement with what's been happening? Have you said "Yes" when "No" was the right answer? Or have you shared your discontent in ineffective ways (gossiping, self-sabotaging, passive-aggressive actions, etc.)? How are you participating in this mistreatment and maintaining the cycle by not standing up for your convictions or enforcing your limits? What pieces of yourself are you giving away, to be liked, accepted, or rewarded?

Once you have a clearer idea of where you stand, reach out for help to get a fresh, informed, yet neutral (outside) perspective. Evaluate this perspective honestly and openly. If it resonates as true, then move on from there. If not, seek another source. Find help that feels right for you, but make sure that you are open to the truth, even if it's difficult to hear.

MOVING FORWARD TO BREAKTHROUGH

✳ STEP BACK

Visualize "Powerful You" defining, expressing, and enforcing your boundaries, displaying your self-respect, and achieving the respect and acceptance of others.

Visualizing the Powerful You

Close your eyes and take three long, deep breaths, relaxing more deeply with each breath.

In your mind's eye, imagine yourself as powerful, strong, authoritative, brimming with self-respect and confidence and easily earning the respect and admiration of others around you.

Envision this empowered version of you (Powerful You) setting appropriate boundaries, enforcing them calmly and unemotionally, expressing herself with ease and self-assurance. See how she is well-respected and like a magnet to others who feel self-acceptance and self-respect.

Now bring to mind the situation in your life in which you feel powerless and disrespected. Ask Powerful You to take charge of the situation.

Observe what she does. Watch as she handles the situation skillfully, with poise, confidence, and authority. See how she speaks to the individuals in charge, those who can affect change, and notice how she wins their respect and trust.

Watch as the outcome of her empowered actions and words unfolds. What becomes possible as a result of her boundary-setting skills?

After the situation is resolved, see her sitting quietly at her desk, appreciating what's occurred and understanding the role she played in bringing about a mutually beneficial outcome.

- From this visualization, what did you learn about the power within you? Consider the boundaries you need to enforce, and how to do it. What shifts in your life and work will be possible when you develop strong boundaries and tap into your self-respect and self-love to enforce them?
- What did Powerful You say and do that was different from what you might have said and done?
- What was the outcome of Powerful You's empowered actions?

✳ **LET GO** of your belief in your powerlessness.

Think about the situation that is causing you the most distress at this time. In your journal, capture all your thoughts. *No censoring, please—write everything that comes to mind.*

- If you knew you were very powerful and could shape the direction of your life in any way you wished, what would you do?
- What would you do if you knew you couldn't fail?
- What would you walk away from or let go of right now?
- What would be different in your life?
- What one step can you take this month to bring out "Powerful You" in your life and work?

✳ **SAY YES!** to developing healthy boundaries.

Recommended Steps

1. Observe this week when you experience intense negative emotions such as anger, resentment, and feeling drained, undervalued, used, or disrespected.

2. Explore all of the situations that generate these emotions. Where do you need to set stronger limits and boundaries? What are you allowing that no longer feels right to you? Who is stepping over or on you, for their purposes?

3. Make a list of what you expect and need from others going forward, as well as what you will no longer accept.

What I need and expect from others: _____

_____

_____

What I will no longer accept: _____

_____

_____

4. Decide what actions you need to take to enforce your new limits. What do you need to do to clearly communicate these boundaries, and to whom?

5. Get support. Find one outside friend, mentor, individual, coach, or organization who can provide a fresh, informed perspective about your current situation. Reach out this week, and share your story.

6. Commit to taking one small step this week to develop your boundaries, honor your limits, and communicate self-love and respect.

Remember

Protecting yourself from injury—of the mind, body, and spirit—is your right and your due in life. But you must claim it. If you feel bruised and beaten up by life and work, don't wait to develop the armor required—your boundaries—to keep you safe and secure. Find an advocate who can show you the way and help you understand how strong you are.

Anne reminds us

"Please don't wait, like I did, for a life-threatening disease to make you walk away from being mistreated. Reach deep inside yourself and find the courage to make a change. Find the strength to do what compels you. If you need to become self-reliant, find a way to do it. If you want to be treated with love, learn how to treat yourself with love. You are far more powerful than you realize. It's not easy to walk away from the cycle, I know, but the rewards are indescribable."

✳ **BREAKTHROUGH** "I am treated with love and respect."

9

Shifting from Competition to Collaboration

The true perfection of man lies not in
what man has, but in what man is. . . .
Nothing should be able to harm a man but
himself. . . . What is outside of him should
be a matter of no importance.

OSCAR WILDE

EMPOWERMENT WITH OTHERS

* **STEP BACK TO EXPLORE** Feeling the need to prove your worth over and over.

* **LET GO** of feeling "not good enough."

* **SAY YES!** to your innate worthiness and value.

* **BREAKTHROUGH**
"I am enough."

* **Robin:** *I have a very competitive spirit that was developed early in my childhood. I was the youngest of four, and the only girl with three older brothers, so there was always a lot of competition. But growing up this way, I never felt different because I was a girl. I wanted to fit in with them—it wasn't even a question. I had to scrap with my brothers in order to win—literally playing with the big boys. Crying or whining never got me anywhere with them. These guys were tough and in order to play (compete), I had to do so on their terms. As I look back, I realize that for me, losing was not an option.*

When I left college and embarked on my career, I was fortunate to choose financial services as a field, because there was great opportunity then (and now). I have continually gravitated to companies with three key environmental factors: the first was a supportive leader and mentor who could guide me, the second was a well-communicated sense of direction and clear-cut vision of what was expected, and the third was the trust that I could get the job done and I could run on my own. Where these factors existed, I have always excelled.

Robin saw early on that in order to survive and fit in with her three brothers, she had to compete, drive hard, quit the whining and complaining, and learn to play on their terms. Losing wasn't an option for her. Many women who've grown up in a male-dominated environment know what Robin means—the feminine aspects of their demeanor, personality, and worldview needed to be downplayed in order to achieve acceptance and respect and to be granted entrance to the "playing field" of their family life. It's no surprise, then, that Robin chose a male-dominated field. It seemed like a perfect fit, and an avenue through which she could utilize all her hard-won skills and savvy. This was a game she knew how to win.

---

* Robin (not her real name) is a 53-year-old senior account manager at a management consultant firm in the financial services industry.

In all my early positions, I worked incredibly hard, achieved well, and gained respect and independence rapidly. I knew how to navigate through these male cultures very well. I gave what was required, and have always been prepared to do so, up until several years ago. Throughout the years, I've been a keen observer of male versus female behavior in the workplace, particularly through nonverbal clues such as attire, behavior, and mannerisms. I've been willing to subordinate my "feminine side"—push it underground—in order to be successful in my role as a management consultant, particularly in the financial services sector, which is so male dominated. This subordination didn't feel wrong to me—I was accustomed to it from my childhood. For instance, when I delivered training courses to groups of men, which I've done extensively, I'd be vigilant to meet them exactly where they were and communicate in ways—both verbally and nonverbally—that encouraged them to hear me and grasp what I was teaching. To do so, I left aspects of my feminine demeanor and personality at the door when I believed these aspects might get in the way.

Throughout my career, I've led, managed, and mentored many younger women, and I realized recently that—please don't judge me for this—I've advised women to downplay their femininity in certain situations where it may be disadvantageous, but also "play up" their female advantages and qualities (in their dress, demeanor, etc.) if their feminine wiles might win a deal or gain an advantage. I didn't see anything wrong with that. I mean, let's face it, don't you think Jack Welch uses his competitive advantage? Of course he does. In order to succeed, I've adopted a "win at all costs" mentality, which worked and fit me well, or so I thought until a few years ago.

In the last several years, this cultural mentality and viewpoint started to break down for me. While I've always been a high achiever, I began to falter because I felt I was not receiving the respect or appreciation that I deserved for my full background and experience, or for what I was bringing to the job. Others—often younger colleagues, many with stronger outside credentials and greater financial achievements in the organization—were climbing ahead of me. This forced me into a competition that made me very uncomfortable. Suddenly, after all these years, I wasn't on top, and didn't want to do what was required to get there (i.e., get a higher degree just for the sake of it). And the more emphasis the company paid to the importance of these external credentials and financial achievements of my younger colleagues (and the more they pitted me against my coworkers), the more fractured and dissatisfied I became. This experience led to my resenting my job, my boss, the company, my fellow workers. Suddenly, I didn't feel like I fit in. I wasn't "winning" at this game, and I questioned if I really wanted to anymore.

What happened then was a confluence of events that turns out was all for the best for me. About a year ago, I came to the realization that none of this was working for me any longer—the environment, the culture, the criteria for success and advancement, the lack of trust, and the misguided leadership. I was very dissatisfied and distressed about how I was being treated at my job, and the resentment I felt for my work, my colleagues, and my superiors was getting in the way of my success. I'd built a twenty-year successful career in this industry, and the staunch competitor in me wasn't ready to walk away from this—that would feel like quitting—like I had "failed." But at the same time, this competitive fervor just wasn't appealing any longer. Plus, my daughters were growing up, and I felt such a longing to be there for them in a deeper way than I had before, to be able to guide them as they navigated through all the challenges of their growing years. I really grappled with what to do. My family needs my full financial contribution, and we've built a life that requires my income. But in the end, I decided enough was enough—I wasn't going to keep playing a game where the rules had changed and I was viewed as holding a losing deck. I was going to take action to address it.

So I decided to articulate some of this to my boss, who became very threatened. In typical form, he wouldn't hear or accept any of what I was telling him, and he resorted to pointing out what he felt were my deficiencies rather than providing guidance or support that would have been instrumental. So I made the challenging move of going above him to his boss to explain my perspective of the situation. He was open and attentive, but in response, the powers that be chose to see that my fit with the organization was no longer ideal and suggested we part ways. This would have been a devastating blow to my ego ten years ago. But now I view it as a good thing . . . a chance to move on as I want to and write another, more fitting, chapter in my life.

I see now that I need to work with people who welcome and embrace my life and business experience, where I am treated as a contributor and collaborator—not as competition for the boss's job or a colleague's job. When work becomes competitive in a destructive fashion—"in order for me to succeed, someone has to fail"—it affects my sense of self-worth and my internal sense of integrity. It breaks down trust in the environment, and I really can't (and don't want to) work any longer where there is a lack of trust and respect.

My idea of worthwhile work is in a job where my full work and life background and experience are considered important to shaping the direction and future of the company. An ideal fit is one where I am a contributor to the greater good of the company, my fellow workers, and the outside world. This view is relatively new for me—that "winning at all costs" is not really winning at all. This alternate view, I think, has emerged in part because of my maturity, my midlife perspective, my growing acceptance of myself, and because of all that I've endured and achieved as a woman and a professional these past twenty years.

Robin describes the arc of her self-discovery in midlife—from a driving competitor who was comfortable and thrived at playing a cut-throat game to win to a maturing, accomplished professional who began to see the effects of this type of competition through another lens. Her new lens was characterized by a focus more aligned with collaboration, respect, integration, inclusion, and appreciation of what she and others could bring to the table than with pitting individuals against each other. Even her decision to share her perspective with her superiors represents a more collaborative, noncompetitive approach—asking for help and support from others when it is called for. The outcome of her act of asking for support and guidance—the organization's request that she leave—gave solid evidence once and for all that Robin had matured and evolved to the point where the fit with the organization was no longer a good one for either of them.

Ego judgments are always made when you meet or work with people. I worked with a guy from Harvard and the one thing we used to joke about was that if you ever met a graduate from Harvard, they will tell you where they went to college in the first twenty words of their introduction! There is some truth to this whether it is overt or not, because it lends perspective to "who you are." Again, in this work culture it's been all about proving your worth through external credentials and validating achievements. These external credentials as measures of success are fine as far as they go, but they don't nearly represent the whole picture, do they? I believe that my whole picture hasn't been fully recognized, and I am seeking to find my next professional role in an environment where the full me—the integration of all my skills, talents, and abilities and aspects—will be taken into account, appreciated, and valued.

My driving ego and the critical judgments I've made toward myself have definitely gotten in the way of feeling satisfied and joyful in my life. My deepest personal critical judgment is that I have a very hard time being "less than perfect." I see it in my work and other people's work. I feel I am always working harder, later, better than everyone else around me. My results are always A+. It is hard to give anything less. As such, I think relationships with coworkers have always been hard. I recognize that my sense of perfection may be hard for others to work with. I am perceived as difficult because I expect the best, no excuses, and I drive hard.

The trade-off for professional women in developing a "winning" attitude for the job is the experience or perception of losing "self" in the process. A sense of "self" for me means that I can be sensitive, caring, introspective and still be successful. Developing my sense of self has taken a very long time. Early in my career it was more important to give up self and "be what they want" me to be—aggressive, driving, strong, and, in the extreme, uncaring or unforgiving. I see now that the sacrifice has been monumental. I gave up friendships, family, satisfying relationships with fellow workers, and an opportunity to enjoy and appreciate myself.

After all this time, I'm finally getting real with the concept that I don't want to compete like this anymore, if it means there's no trust, respect, collaboration, or integration. I still grapple with the question "Is getting real the same as 'giving up'?" I'm still not 100 percent sure because the driving competitor in me has been there for so many years. Of course I am asking this tongue in cheek . . . but it is amazing that it took a few decades for me to realize that one can work productively and minimize the competition element. But it is not entirely removed.

As I have gotten older, I view the competition is now from younger workers. I do believe we have bent the paradigm and the traditional male workplace sees more than it used to the value of women and diversity in the workplace. But at the same time, I recognize that the traditional workplace is not for me anymore. My goals and values have changed dramatically, and what I want from my work is larger than "playing the game" and giving up my personal sense of integrity.

Robin's story reveals a critical lesson—often, what we want so desperately in our twenties and thirties is not at all what we end up desiring later in life. This change is not a bad thing, or something to bemoan or regret. This is life. Many midlife individuals look at their decisions and life choices and regret them because they feel so unhappy or thwarted in their current situation. But they fail to understand that what they chose for themselves in the past was most likely in perfect alignment with who they were *then*. They've simply grown and changed. Midlife does that to you. Robin isn't saying that driving competition is wrong. Nor is she negatively judging others for wanting to win. She's simply saying that it's wrong for her *now*.

Robin shows us what it means to accept life change in a positive, fluid way. Avoiding regret when looking back at your choices is vitally important. Regret is destructive because it reinforces how stuck you feel, and then allows you to beat yourself up for it. Starting today, let go of regret, all of it. Remember that each of us is doing the best s/he can in every moment. If you don't like where you are today, don't look back. Look forward, address any wrongs you feel you've done to yourself and others, and take action to change your path.

Robin says of her life now: *Clarity only comes from being separated from the situation, and never was this more true than now. I've left my last job that was so unfulfilling and difficult, and this time away has made all the difference. It was important to develop my sense of what I want beyond monetary goals. I've explored and examined, "What was I giving up to work at this job? What sacrifices to my family, my life, my time, my personal values did I make?" The answers have been chilling, but I'm ready to move forward.*

I've overcome my need to win at all costs, and I'm so looking forward to helping other women get to this point in their careers, sooner than I did, or bypass that type of thinking altogether. I don't want to sublimate parts of myself any longer, and I realize I simply don't have to. That was the old way. I'm ready for the new way and won't say no until I carve it out for myself. I am focused on the big picture and how I can contribute to the greater good. I want to be in an environment where I know I am giving back to the community and where I can use my experience and on-the-job knowledge to build the community.

Personally, this transition involved taking an honest inventory of my skills, my experience, my successes and developing stories about who I am and what I have to offer in an integrated and full-view way. In the process I realized I am quite a special woman with great skills and experience that cannot be taught in college.

Understanding this intersection of where I want to be and what I have to offer has actually led me to pursue new roles in community development, on nonprofit boards, and in mentoring. I recognize that I have had angels in my life and that if I carry a positive attitude and share what I have to offer, I can be an angel in someone else's life. And I can be a role model for my growing daughters that "winning" doesn't have to mean losing your sense of self and your integrity in the process. That's what matters most to me now.

ROBIN'S ADVICE

- Heal feeling not good enough, and let go of your negative ego judgments.
- Look at the cost of "winning at all costs."
- Get real—you don't want to play this game anymore.

Heal Feeling "Not Good Enough"

What does it mean to "win" in business, in our careers, in life? Does it mean someone has to fail, look bad, or lose for us to succeed? Of course, competition can be healthy and positive, but then again, it can be damaging and limiting.

Over the years I've met many individuals who are overly competitive. They simply cannot feel any level of comfort or joy at being collaborative, inclusive, or accepting—they must always be "on top." Do you know such people? Are you like this yourself? Relating and connecting with these individuals always feels like a tough competition, a one-upping game rather than a comfortable, easy, authentic sharing and connecting. Many overly competitive individuals can't accept dissent, challenge, or diversity. They see everything and everyone in terms of a relative hierarchy or pecking order. No matter what these folks have achieved or earned, at their core they feel simply not yet good enough. So they keep striving, slaving to be the "best." But the best never comes.

Feeling not good enough leads people to be highly critical of themselves and others. Their thoughts are constantly full of judgments, about who is better, worse, smarter, sexier, more successful, more popular, more capable, and so on. These continual, critical judgments foster insecurity, fear, and imbalance. When you are addicted to judging others and comparing yourself to them, it means you're addicted to judging yourself, and to finding fault and imperfection everywhere you look.

If you feel you are good at work and life only when you're "ahead" of everyone else, then something within you is longing for acceptance, validation, and attention. If you feel you're only as good as your last deal, win, performance, or paycheck—and can't feel good enough without these outside ego achievements—then life will deliver an opportunity. In whatever form benefits you most, you'll have a chance to accept and value yourself in the face of not winning, not succeeding, and not dominating.

Feeling not good enough *prevents* you from being able to do the following with success and satisfaction:

- Connect deeply with others
- Feel compassion and empathy
- Develop and maintain successful relationships
- Feel good in the face of challenge and adversity
- Accept yourself in loving ways
- Be of heartfelt service to others

- Take risks
- Step up to the life or career change you want because you feel you may fail
- Feel relaxed, centered, and in the moment
- Have quick access to joy

Feeling not good enough holds you back and keeps you stuck. If you experience any aspect of this, it's time to heal that gap and move forward to celebrating good enough, in yourself and your work. After all, "good enough" is often just perfect.

Look at the Cost of Winning at All Costs

Winning at all costs often ends up feeling like losing. If you've had to give up your soul, integrity, values, and priorities to come out on top, then *who you are* has become less important than what you do/achieve/earn. Who you *are* is far more significant, powerful, and lasting than any outside achievement or thing. Who you are each day is what will be remembered about you, long after your achievements have faded. What matters most is a strong positive concept and understanding of yourself and your intrinsic value, which allows you to feel good and worthwhile no matter what is happening around you, no matter what deal you've lost or gaping mistake you've made. Winning at all costs requires losing yourself along the way, and becoming cut off from your internal compass that guides you to be all you are meant to be. When you have given up so much to win something outside yourself (job, title, money, accolades, deals, material items), sadness and loss often come, because outside objects can't be retained forever. These external rewards will somehow become elusive, or someone new will come up the ranks to steal them from you.

Get Real—You Don't Want to Play This Game Anymore

Robin's life dramatically changed when she realized that playing this competitive game no longer appealed to her. She got real with herself and faced the startling fact that she wasn't "winning" any longer, and didn't really care to. Many women in midlife have found that pitting themselves against others just doesn't feel right or worthwhile anymore. Instead of focusing on how people are better or worse than others, these women have chosen to bring forward a more inclusive, expansive framework for life and work that recognizes individuals for their unique talents and experience. Whether this shift is due to a midlife reevaluation, maturity, or an evolution in perspective, women are walking away from believing they are only as good as their last success, deal, or win.

Robin came to this realization at the same time as she shifted toward wanting to be there in a more connected way for her daughters. This is not a coincidence. "And" thinking—a perspective that fosters inclusion, diversity, and acceptance—affects all aspects of our lives. "And" thinking brings about opportunity, growth, and movement, whereas "or" thinking creates limitations, conflict, fear, and inertia. Which type of thinker are you?

MOVING FORWARD TO BREAKTHROUGH

✷ STEP BACK

To determine if you are endeavoring to "win at all costs," ask yourself the following questions:

• Do I feel good about myself?	Yes	No
• Do I have my integrity in what I'm doing and how I'm living?	Yes	No
• Do I feel that I am a positive force in the world?	Yes	No
• Do I feel worthy of respect, from myself and others?	Yes	No
• Do I feel worthwhile and valuable, despite what others say?	Yes	No

If you answered "No" to any of these questions, perhaps you are feeling driven to compete to know that you are valuable in life. If you believed that you are worthwhile and important, just being who you are, without winning, what changes would you make in life and work?

Think about:

- How would I feel if I walked away from this competition?
- What have I given up in order to win at this job, this career, this life?
- When I'm 90 years old, looking back, will I say that what I've achieved was worth what I gave up?

✳ **LET GO** of feeling "not good enough."

In your journal, capture all your thoughts. *No censoring, please—write everything that comes to mind.*

- In what areas in your life do you feel "not good enough"?
- What specifically makes you feel this way?
- From where/who do you think you received the message that you are not good enough?
- What would happen if, for once, you allowed "good enough" to be perfect?
- Who can serve as your role model for living and working in a balanced, successful, competent, open, secure manner, who also embodies an "I am good enough" acceptance of herself/ himself?
- Where can you try in your life and work being *simply good enough* (not perfect, not the best, not the winner)? Where can you intentionally walk away from the game, try not to win, and give yourself evidence that you will survive not being the winner each moment, in each situation?
- What actions can you take this month to step away from your driving need for perfectionism and competition, and celebrate yourself as good enough?

✳ **SAY YES!** to your innate worthiness and value.

Recommended Steps

1. Find a place to sit quietly, relaxed, comfortable, undisturbed. Take three long, deep breaths, relaxing more deeply with each breath.
2. Now close your eyes, and bring to mind a time from the past when you felt valuable, worthwhile, accepted, and loved. Bring it fully to your mind's eye, and remember all the details of the situation. What were you doing, being? Who were you with? Who was showing you acceptance, love, respect, and admiration, and for what reasons? How specifically did you experience this acceptance and validation?
3. Write down all of the qualities you were displaying during that time. What were you revealing or expressing that brought out others' admiration, acceptance, and love of you? Were you winning a competitive game? Or were you connecting

with others, helping people, being yourself, showing your innate gifts and abilities, being bold, or insightful, or funny, or artistic?

4. Make a list of all your qualities that are valuable, lovable, respectable, worthy of admiration. (Make this list as long as you can—include everything, no matter how small.)

5. Finally, review your list of what you believe makes you a human being of value, worth, importance, and significance. Are you living these qualities? Is your day full of expressing these traits and qualities, or is your life and work about suppressing them?

6. Take action this month to bring forward all of your traits and characteristics that you believe reveal your worth, your value, your gifts, and your specialness, as a human being on this planet today.

Remember

Competition is fine if you are *thriving* in it, and enjoying yourself and your life, and who you've become in the process. If you aren't, it's time to reassess what you have given up to win. It's time to embrace that "good enough" is, at the right time, just perfect.

Robin reminds us

"After all this time, I'm finally getting real with the concept that I don't want to compete anymore, if it means there's no trust, respect, collaboration, or integration. It took me a few decades to realize that one can work productively and minimize the competition element. My goals and values have changed dramatically, and what I want from my work is larger than 'playing the game' and giving up my personal sense of integrity."

✳ **BREAKTHROUGH** "I am enough."

EMPOWERMENT WITH THE WORLD

10

Escaping
Financial Traps

Do not value money for any more
nor any less than its worth; it is
a good servant but a bad master.

ALEXANDRE DUMAS

✳ **Amanda:** *I worked for a very challenging company for eighteen years, and I went through some exhausting trials and tribulations with them. From highly visible and nerve-wracking lawsuits to incompetent bosses to an employee turnover rate of more than 30 percent in a single year due to gross mismanagement, I endured my time there, toughed it out, in part because I felt that my role was important and helpful to people. But if I look back honestly, I think I really stayed because I had started on this path and didn't know how to get off. I continued to get promoted, making more and more money. I also kept getting more responsibilities, so the job was never boring. I think the great salary, promotions, new responsibilities, and perks just kept me there. The job wasn't a good fit for me, but it made possible some things that I felt were important, like a nice house, lovely clothes, a tennis club membership, travel, freedom and financial independence from my parents and others, etc. It's funny, I'm not a materialistic person overall, but I was so focused on doing my job well every day, building a strong and secure career for myself, and living this life I'd created (with its heavy obligations to a host of family and friends), that I never stopped to examine how unfulfilling and stressful my life was. I didn't see my relationships too clearly, either. I missed the fact that so many people were using and draining me, and many weren't capable of giving back at all. I feel like I was so busy living my life that I wasn't conscious of what I was missing—a career that thrills me, fulfilling relationships, and utilizing my creative talents.*

Then, after being offered a different position with extensive travel, which I turned down, I was laid off, and I decided to make a huge change. I'd always adored music and theater and was very knowledgeable about the theatrical world, so I decided to take the plunge and pursue being a music producer. This wasn't a lark—I was deeply committed to this and knew a great deal about the field, and I felt this was the right move for me. I spent six years on this road, working with various producers, learning the craft, scoping out new talent, representing great vocalists and their recordings, attending hundreds of shows and performances. I absolutely loved all of it. The problem was that I didn't make any money. I kept finding new great talent and exciting new projects, but the money didn't come. I simply ran out. Nothing substantial was coming in, and I couldn't pay my bills. It was so grueling, scary, and isolating . . . to be without money and unable to pay my debts. I'd never experienced that before. I even had to get some help from the very people in my life from whom I'd worked so hard to gain independence.

I come from parents of European descent, and they came from literally nothing. My mother was from a very poor family that had to scrape to eat. My parents are self-made, and they did tremendously well in their financial endeavors here. From this background, and growing up in a very affluent town, I guess I developed the thinking that having money was paramount, nonnegotiable, a given. I'd always been able to make good money . . . I took that fact for granted. So when I went out on a limb and pursued a new direction professionally, I never expected that I wouldn't make good money at it. Never. But I didn't. At a certain point, I knew I just couldn't go on. The money worries took over. I went through a very stressful time of asking myself, "Now what? What should I do? Do I walk away from producing, which I absolutely love and am great at, and turn my back on all I've done these past years?"

After struggling so long without money, I knew I needed a change, so I found a job in a field related to my corporate job. I didn't want to do this particular work at all, but I felt I had little choice. Quickly on, I saw that it was a terrible fit. The people, the work itself, the office dynamics, the way I was treated, and the pay . . . none of it worked. And then, just at the end of the year, my boss cut my salary dramatically, and I knew I had to leave. But after this experience, something shifted inside me, something big. I woke up somehow. I became very focused and sure of one thing. I said, "I've got to make a change here. I've got to earn money, pay off my debts, but still do something that's rewarding and enjoyable. I'm not going to give up on music producing, but I've got to take control."

Amanda's story tells of the deeply challenging experience of being disempowered by money in two potent but different ways. First, her original career that gave her financial success and security was grueling, stressful, and draining. It didn't give her the chance to pursue her true lifelong loves—the arts, performance, music, and theater. She earned great money but wasn't able to focus on what she deeply valued and treasured. Second,

Amanda experienced agonizing fear when money failed to materialize. She lived in constant dread that the money wouldn't come, and her worst fears came true—it didn't. Either way, money had the upper hand in Amanda's life.

Your Relationship with Money

Allowing money to be our master is one of the most serious errors of our time. It's an epidemic. Many of us believe that money will cure all ills, keep us safe, bring us luck, power, and esteem, make us beautiful, fulfill us, and make it okay that we're not doing what we long to. Money can be numbing, like a narcotic. I've worked with individuals whose shopping addiction is as destructive as a severe drug addiction.

Many folks today speak of money the way people in ancient times spoke of their ferocious gods. Money must be fed and feared, revered as the master. It seems that we continually give money our gifts of sacrifice, like lambs on an altar, just to remain in its favor. We offer up our talents, our longings, and our souls, praying to be spared hardship and suffering. If we hold money in higher esteem than ourselves and our creative spirits, it will control us.

However, if we take money for granted, as something that always flows automatically, we miss seeing the true meaning of the situation: Money, and how you feel when you are making and spending it, is a form of energy. The way it flows and feels relates to your own sense of worth, security, and strength in the world.

To be fair, I've seen many people make beautiful magic with their money. I've met inspiring individuals who have turned their hardships and personal suffering into global endeavors that change the world for the better. Theresa Wilson, founder of The Blessing Basket Project® (www.blessingbasket.org), is one of these individuals (see chapter 13). Many creative individuals use their money and talents to bring glorious and moving pieces of visual art, music, and literature to the world. Clearly, money can make possible an expanded experience of joy, beauty, and goodness.

What separates people who have a joyful relationship with money from those who don't? People who are successful and joyful in their money relationships are generally empowered in other aspects of life as well. As Maria Nemeth discusses in her insightful book *The Energy of Money*,[1] money is one of six vital energy forms, along with time, physical vitality, enjoyment, creativity, and support of friends. How you are with money also reflects the quality of your relationships with other key energy forms.

With regard to money, I've observed a number of key tendencies.

Money tends to flow joyfully and easily when:

- You are in balance as a creative individual and can adjust positively to changes in your outside world.
- You know that you are valuable, good, and important, despite what's happening around you.
- You avoid being overly committed to a single facet or dimension of yourself.
- You take actions that reflect a positive, all-encompassing view of yourself.
- You feel respected and valued in your relationships.
- You know *you* guide your life and can modify your course when things aren't working.
- You view money as a positive, affirming element.
- You have clear ideas of the good you will do with your money for yourself, others, and the world.

Money tends to stop flowing joyfully and easily when:

- You're out of balance and react negatively to change.
- You carry beliefs that you are bad or inadequate, and you worry about others' negative opinions of you.
- You have strong attachments to how things "should be" and what you "deserve" rather than being able to live and learn from how things are now.
- You act from fear and doubt and behave in ways that limit you.
- Your relationships with others are strained, resistant, and conflictual.
- You blame others or outside circumstances for your problems with money.
- You believe that having money is somehow bad, dirty, or selfish.
- You don't know what good you'd do with money, if you had it.

Focusing solely on your lack of money will lead to being driven by fear, worry, and self-doubt. You won't be able to see the options available to you or the positive directions you could take. Conversely, if you generate abundant money but are overly focused on the material items it affords, you're allowing something outside yourself to make life enjoyable and meaningful. Either way, money rules.

If you are struggling with money, I recommend that you take a look at how you feel about money in general, and how you relate to it. Rebalancing and strengthening your internal relationship with money now will help you create a more satisfying financial experience in the future.

But positive thinking isn't enough to turn things around. We have to take action that helps us step up to be the person we long to be. If being in debt feels terrible to you, figure out how to reduce your debt and do it. If working part-time in another field would give you access to health benefits that you desperately need, say yes! to a job that you feel good about. Do what you need to feel balanced, hopeful, and powerful in your relationship with money, and positive results will follow.

Amanda continues: *From that point on, things have been different. I sought employment in an HR-related field that I'd had previous experience in, but I made sure to find a position that was going to work on my terms. It's very flexible, and I can act independently, earn a healthy commission, and apply the particular HR skills that I enjoy utilizing (versus many of my previous tasks and responsibilities that felt like chores). I'm connected to a successful firm with a great reputation that I could be excited to work for. Before I took the job, I met several of my colleagues, and I was impressed with them and with what they said about the organization. My boss seemed to be great and was well thought of, too. I felt like this could be a solution that was more than feasible for me, for the time being, allowing me to support my creative side while doing professional work that I enjoy. I've been there six months now, and I really like it. I am great at the work, I find the people stimulating, and I feel respected for my talents. I'm one of the top performers, and I like it!*

I know that this job isn't forever, but becoming more solvent and paying off my debts now feels right. I'm much more secure and confident now that I've taken charge of my life. I'm not going to give up on my dream of producing—I've come too far for that—but I know I need patience. I'm on a career journey that allows me to pay my bills and address my debts, but also commit other available hours to producing music, which is my dream. This job allows me to use the skills and talents I truly enjoy, while being very flexible and independent. I keep working toward my creative goals and am developing several music projects while making a living that keeps me engaged and afloat. My relationships with people have changed for the better, too. I simply don't have time for people who drain me or take for granted that I'll be there for them, when they're not there for me. I've slowly cleared away things and relationships that don't support me. My life is working well for me now, and I feel really good about the direction I'm heading in.

AMANDA'S ADVICE

- Do what's required to feel balanced about money. Take action that allows you to handle your debts well, but do it consciously. Let work represent important aspects of who you are, even if it's not the ideal situation yet.
- Know the creative endeavors you want in your life and make sure they are represented. Don't give up on your creative dreams. Keep working on them. If they're important enough to you, you'll find a way.
- Clear away people and relationships that drain you and bring you down.

Balance Your Relationship with Money

What is a healthy, balanced relationship with money? From my view, it involves earning (and having access to) all the money you *truly* need and want, while acting in a way that brings you a sense of purpose, accomplishment, and integrity. Balance with regard to money implies that the relationship is one of equality and respect—that money facilitates your efforts to be and do what you wish to, in life and work. Money allows you to share with the world who you are and what matters to you. Money is not the end result, nor does it possess any particular qualities or traits in and of itself. It is simply an energy form. Money is the means through which you can either expand yourself or limit yourself. If viewed and handled positively, money allows you to apply your unique capabilities and gifts in and for the world.

Clients have come to me confused and desperate about money, often explaining that their businesses and professional endeavors have been disastrous financially. Other clients who make tremendous money feel like they are selling their soul for financial security, as I did for many years. In working with these individuals, over time we uncover a myriad of ingrained beliefs about money that are negative, restrictive, or fear-based. My negative thinking about money led me to believe that I would always make great money but would have to give up my soul and dreams to do it. It has taken me years to revise this one destructive belief. But I'm committed to acting from an empowered view that is money is not the enemy. My new framework is "I am able to generate abundant money while doing soul-enriching work."

What are your beliefs about money? How are you acting and living that keeps you subservient to and fearful about money?

Know What You Long to Do and Honor It with Balance

Amanda uncovered a deep longing to work in the music industry, as a producer and developer of projects and talent. This creative longing powerfully emerged after she was laid off from her long-term corporate career. I've seen this over and over—after years of drudgery and pain of doing work that doesn't fit, something snaps and we awaken to creative or soulful longings that won't be denied. Honoring our creative longings is vital; it is a positive and essential aspect of a satisfying life. But it's critical to honor these longings *all along the way*, with conscious thought and empowered action. Following our desires can turn destructive if we end up becoming a servant to them. Balance is everything. Creative and spiritual longings are within us from the beginning of our lives, but we often ignore them. When disregarded, these desires finally break free and demand urgently to be addressed. But urgency begets imbalance.

I broke down from having to navigate through dehumanizing corporate political warfare. I was desperate to find a new work path that would help people. This spiritual longing emerged so fiercely that I neglected everything else in order to immerse myself in my psychotherapy studies. The problem with this shift was that my family's standard of living required me to earn a sizable income, and I had stopped doing so. I continued to earn insufficient money for years, in blind stubbornness—refusing to change our lifestyle yet not able to support it. In becoming a slave to doing good, I was neglecting both my other responsibilities to the family and other productive dimensions of myself (the successful business professional, the effective leader, the wise money manager, etc.). I was unrealistic, too, about how long it would take me to earn the money I needed and wanted to in my new career. I didn't listen to the solid advice I was given, that a full, self-sustaining private practice would most likely take five or so years to develop. "Not for me." I thought. "I'll do it much quicker!" Turns out I was wrong.

A better, more balanced approach that would have reduced my stress and freed up some much-needed energy would have been to 1) get out of denial and face my financial realities head-on, and 2) get part-time, stable work (with health benefits, if possible!) in an organization related to my new field. This approach would have helped me pay my bills while also expanding my skills as a therapist and coach.

People sometimes ask me, "How long should I keep this up, following my dream?"

I typically respond, "If you can consider giving it up, then most likely you're not really committed to giving it everything you've got." Following your dreams requires guts and an amazing amount of tenacity, courage, perseverance, and patience. If you can foresee giving up on the dream, maybe it's not for you after all. In other words, figure out what you *can't live without doing*, and do that. But do it consciously, with balance.

Even when following your dreams, focusing on only one dimension to the exclusion of all others (in my case, my spiritual longings and in Amanda's, her creative desires) leads us to act in out-of-control ways. Other needs in your life must also be addressed through balanced action—paying your bills, saving for the future, protecting your health and welfare and that of your family, and so on. The goal is to honor your creative and spiritual longings in balanced ways *while* addressing your financial needs so you feel secure.

Various approaches to getting the financial support you need exist:

- Consult with a reputable financial consultant, who can assist you in evaluating your financial situation and making solid plans for your transition and your future.
- Get advice from respected experts in your field about what you'd like to do, an estimated time frame for achieving it, and the skills, education, and tools required to succeed (and listen to the advice!).
- Participate in workshops and seminars on financial planning given by local or national organizations (such as the chamber of commerce, a local library, women's business development centers, SCORE, and Make Mine a Million Dollar Business), and learn about grants, scholarships, and loans available for women.
- Develop a solid business plan for your new endeavor, with guidance from the above-mentioned organizations or individuals.
- Study several of the hundreds of terrific resources on financial planning and money management (I recommend Suze Orman, David Bach, and David Ramsey's books, for starters).
- Ask someone you know who is powerful and effective in her money management skills to mentor you and provide ongoing guidance.

Addressing your financial needs along with your other needs and longings will ensure that your life continues to flow from a centered, secure place and is reflective of the many dimensions of you. Money thus becomes a form of support and enrichment for your integrated life—no more, no less.

Shed What Keeps You Down

Amanda describes the quality of her relationships both before and after taking control of her life and honoring her needs and longings. Before, many of her friends and family seemed to take advantage of her, assuming that she'd be there for them through their troubles, yet they were unwilling to support and nurture her when she needed it. She felt a servant to many relationships and situations that weren't healthy or positive for her.

After gaining a clear understanding of what she wanted in life—to honor her creative desires while attending to the business of managing her life constructively—she shed things and relationships that were draining, negative, and unsupportive. Now she simply doesn't have time or energy for things that keep her down and small. She's outgrown them.

Honoring all that you are in life takes a great deal of energy, time, focus, and commitment. To do so, we need people who encourage and invigorate us. Here's a useful question to ask yourself in evaluating who in your life is helpful and who is not: *"Does this person want me to be all I can be in life, based on my definition? Is s/he capable of supporting me on this new path?"* If the answer is "No," then some clearing may be necessary. If you want to move away from some people and relationships that are holding you back, you may wish to get outside support and guidance on how best to proceed. A coach or therapist can be a great place to start. To find a coach in your area, visit www.coachfederation.org. For a directory of marriage and family therapists in your area, check out www.aamft.org.

MOVING FORWARD TO BREAKTHROUGH

✳ STEP BACK

To gain awareness of your beliefs about money, in your journal, capture all your thoughts. *No censoring, please—write everything that comes to mind.*

- Think back to when you were a child. What messages were you told by your parents and other important authority figures about money? What did you learn about having or not having money, the importance of it, the power of it, the desirability of it? List those messages in your journal.

- What *new* beliefs have you developed about money in your adult years? Write them down.
- Looking over all the thoughts you hold about money, identify those that feel restrictive, negative, or critical or are based on insecurity or lack. Cross out those that feel negative.
- What new, positive thoughts can you create about money and what it will bring to your life? What positive outcomes will come—to you, your family, others, and the world—when money flows to you as you hope? (For instance: I'll take family vacations that create beautiful memories; I'll beautify my home; I'll protect the health of my family; I'll take time off to relax; I'll finally write my book, etc.). Write them down.
- Review this list of positive outcomes daily. Look for evidence that these outcomes and positive beliefs about money are valid and true for you and will in fact come to pass.

✳ LET GO of beliefs, relationships, and actions that keep you small.

In your journal, capture all your thoughts. *No censoring, please—write everything that comes to mind.*

- Think about the key people in your life today. List them.
- For each, ask yourself: Does this person want me to be all I can be in life and work? Is s/he able and willing to support me on my new path? If the answer to these questions is "No," think about how you can empower yourself to protect your longings and desires and keep them safe and supported. (Seek the help of a therapist, coach, women's group, or other support networks.)
- In what situations do you feel "smaller" (less powerful) than you wish to?
- What one step can you take today that will help you regain power in these situations? How can you achieve balance?

✳ SAY YES! to a balanced relationship with money.

Recommended Steps
1. Quietly go inward and ask yourself—consult your inner guidance, your intuition—to explore taking affirming action in regard to money.

- What needs to be done now in your money situation that would make you feel more empowered and in control?
- What holds you back from doing these things?

2. Accepting for a moment that improving your money relationship is in your hands, brainstorm what you would be able to do this month to

  - Feel better about money
  - Earn more money
  - Save more money
  - Manage your money more wisely
  - Be more powerful, loving, and balanced in your relationship with money
  - Enjoy money

3. Commit to taking one important step this month to gain control and self-confidence in your relationship with money.

Remember

Money is energy that flows when you flow. Connect with what you long to do, balance that consciously with what you need to do, and let money be a helper, supporter, and respected friend. Clear away beliefs and actions that keep you angry, resistant, and un-supported. It's up to you to do this, and you can.

Amanda reminds us

"Taking full charge of my life feels great. For once, I am balancing what I long to do with what I need to do, and I'm good with it. I believe with all my heart that I will have ev-erything I dream of—a fulfilling career, great relationships, creative projects that excite me, and a lifestyle that means joy, freedom, and independence. Believing in my dreams, and taking action that supports me and what I need, has changed everything."

✳ **BREAKTHROUGH** "I fulfill my financial needs and honor who I am."

11

Using Real Talents
in Life and Work

*Man is the only creature
who refuses to be what he is.*

ALBERT CAMUS

EMPOWERMENT WITH THE WORLD

✳ **STEP BACK TO EXPLORE** Denying the power of your unique gifts.

✳ **LET GO** of your fears of failure and inadequacy.

✳ **SAY YES!** to believing in your talents without fail.

✳ **BREAKTHROUGH**

"I use my real talents in life and work."

✳ **Monique:** *When I think back to my childhood, I never really seized on a specific career path that I wanted. But from when I was a little girl, I thought about being a performer of some sort, maybe a singer. I didn't have a great childhood. It was marred by a lot of instability and insecurity. So I knew I wanted security and stability, and I wasn't picky about how I'd accomplish that.*

The first major decision I made in life was not to finish college. I was studying accounting, but I found the whole thing so boring. I remember somebody said to me then that cosmetics would always be great business, so I left college and got my first job at Estée Lauder. I loved it and was good at it because it was immediate and it helped people. I did very well, working there from age 18 to 24.

Then something happened that changed my life. I had married my high school sweetheart, and after about a year and half, he ran off with another woman. I wasn't quite 24 years old when I got divorced for the first time. That experience threw me into an odd sort of depression—I felt suddenly purposeless and empty. While I loved cosmetics, I felt it had no real value for me. I felt compelled to seek a deeper, more profound thing to do with my life, to give me the security I longed for. Being married to my high school sweetheart was the thing that had given my life meaning up until that point. I had taken the track that "nice Latin girls" take, and I had thought it was the right thing for me, but I realized I was wrong.

I then toyed with the idea of going back to school, but I knew I was a good salesperson and people liked me. So I went to a temporary employment service to help me regroup and find a way out of retail. I went into a position of underwriting medical malpractice insurance policies, and it turned out I was really good at it. But the company I worked for asked me to stop associating with a former employee who was a close personal friend, so after a period of refusing to do that, I got fired.

I was home one day watching TV, and Oprah *came on. Something about seeing her show affected me deeply. I sat there for hours after and wrote this long manifesto about my life called "The End of Slavehood." In it, I detailed for myself all that I hated about my previous work life, and the things I would never succumb to again. From that point on, I knew I needed to be independent, so I formed my own corporation, Marvez and Madison, and worked for my girlfriend's company selling medical malpractice insurance. I continued doing this for three years, and at 27 years old I was doing well and making some very decent money. But after a while, I begin to contemplate what my life's big picture was and wondered if this was it. I hoped not.*

As Monique discovered after "trying on" several different professional identities, being good at your work simply isn't enough to build a happy, fulfilling life, not if the work doesn't match who you are. What's required for a satisfying and genuinely meaningful life is something else—discovering what you're naturally and joyfully gifted at, and stepping forward to do work that makes use of these gifts. Women often realize, after following a secure but joyless road for years, that life will happen, and traumas emerge, including exploitation, loss, disappointment, and sudden negative shifts away from what they anticipated. Sometimes these shifts are "just life," but more often than not they have a purpose, which is to point you—like a red neon sign in the road—to follow a more authentic, self-affirming direction, one that allows you to honor what you've been endowed with and use your core gifts.

Monique continues: *It's funny, big things often happen to me after a terrible illness. I don't believe in illness per se—I call it the "grievels," when something is dying or changing or shifting, because changing makes you grieve when you have to move on. It was May, and I was really sick with a terrible cold and fever. Lying in bed reading the paper, I saw an article about Sam Kinison that mentioned he had played in Miami the night before. The photo showed him walking out of the arena with a buxom blonde on each arm, and I thought, "If that big fat bastard is getting rich and laid by doing stand-up, I'm going to try it!"*

In the article, I saw a local comedy club mentioned, and I just picked up the phone and called the club out of the blue. I said, "How do you do comedy there?" and they told me. I said, "Okay, I want to come tomorrow." I was onstage the next night. I had been onstage performing a lot in school plays, so I was really comfortable in the spotlight. I thought about funny things I'd said over the years, sitting in a Denny's with my girlfriends, and cobbled together some funny moments to make an act. After the set, the owner came up to me and said, "You're a natural. Come back next week."

And that was the start of my comedy career. It was that simple. I'd never been a comedy groupie, but my whole life, my friends have said, "You should be a comedian, you're a riot!!" I didn't think I was funny, but I knew I was brutally honest, and said out loud what other people just think to themselves.

Following Our Natural Gifts

From her childhood, Monique emerged with the dominant wish to create security and stability for herself. This longing governed her career decisions and led her to seek professional paths that initially looked like they'd give her what she wanted, but they disappointed her each time.

Finally, she had an awakening and was compelled, almost by something outside herself, to pursue comedy. Her stunning natural gifts came together in a perfect blend—spreading laughter, using her wordsmith gift, loving the spotlight, applying her uncanny powers of observation, speaking her wildly funny mind, and taking full advantage of all she is (gloriously not skinny, not blonde). But not until the "grievels" took hold of her did she realize that she could use those talents in a career.

Women often disregard or underestimate the importance of their natural gifts and talents. They chronically fail to recognize ways in which they are unique and special, or to understand that these gifts exist for one key reason—to use them in the world, and to bring joy. Further, being driven to find security and stability means that we are motivated by *fear*—fear that we will be forced to experience the same trauma we did in childhood. Or we fear breaking away from the tribal mentality we were raised with. But submitting to fear inevitably leads to actions that bring suffering or discontent.

When I was a teen, I knew I loved to sing and perform, and I had evidence that I was good at it. I also knew that I took great pleasure in writing, as well as in exploring why humans do what they do. Being a compassionate listener to people in need was another natural talent I enjoyed. These are my natural gifts and abilities—compassionate listening, understanding human behavior, using my voice to connect with and assist people, and entertaining—all of which come together to help me do what I love best.

Why, then, did it take me twenty years to find "right" work for myself? Why did I take so long to draw on these talents? Because I failed to see my unique gifts. I didn't believe these natural talents that I love to use would be the best building blocks for a successful, satisfying career and life. Instead, I pursued a series of jobs that represented money and security but were boring or unfulfilling to me. Only after a series of seemingly random traumatic and disruptive events did I wake up and stop working solely for security. I finally figured out that my natural gifts and talents could be used to forge a career path I could sink my teeth into.

Monique's Journey Through Comedy

So I committed myself to comedy. For years, I took every gig I was offered, traveled across the country, and loved performing. The problem was I made very little money and I was always broke. Everyone told me I should quit, but I knew in my heart I couldn't. After my second marriage ended, I said, "Okay, something's got to change here." I'm a spiritual person and I pray a lot, but I don't know whence the answers come. There's something bigger out there, so I started asking, "Am I crazy? Have I mixed my wires? Why is this such a struggle?" I felt like this was the one huge thing I do that makes me special, so I've got to do it. But I kept asking questions, doubting, and wondering, "Should I quit?" until something finally happened that gave me the answer I was looking for.

It was February 2002, and I needed money desperately. After a brutally honest conversation with a friend who said, "Your life is ridiculous! You're always flat broke!" I thought that this really might be the end of the line for me and comedy. As luck would have it, my next gig was in Oklahoma for a wonderful woman named Dixie who loved me and always hired me when I was passing through. I used to sell T-shirts after my shows and would tell people I'd give them a one-minute psychic reading for the price of the T-shirt. This wasn't a power trip. I'm very intuitive, and I'd know things about their lives. So at this gig, I was asked to do a reading.

One guy in the audience had been in a terrible motorcycle wreck. He was disfigured, missing an eye, really torn up. I started to read him, and out of nowhere I began saying, "You have to apologize and start talking to God. You can try every way possible to kill yourself, but you're going to survive, because you don't have that power. Whether you like it or not, you're not going to die." He said to me, "I wouldn't even know where to begin to talk to God." And I responded, "Just go out to an open field and look up, and say, 'I'm listening.' I told him he was very powerful, special, and that he'd been kept alive because he had something to say that was important. You could see a shift literally right there in his face. He thanked me, left the bar, and for a moment everybody there was completely stunned, silent, just looking around in awe.

That was it. From that second on, I knew I couldn't quit. I made up my mind to never give up on this life of comedy and performing, and when I did that, I felt better. From that day forward to this, wonderful, miraculous events have occurred in my life. A year after that evening at Dixie's bar, I heard from an amazing L.A. entertainment attorney, Jeffrey, who was interested in representing me and collaborating. We met and instantly connected, and I saw that he believed in me as powerfully as anyone ever could. He's my manager now, and we work beautifully together. Soon after that, I was offered my own radio show, which was a terrific run. Despite the fact that I'm not skinny or blonde, and everyone told me I had to be to make it, I moved back to L.A. for the third time. Just one day after arriving, I performed at an HBO showcase and was approached by Dick Wolf Entertainment to work with them to create, develop, and star in my own network pilot! And it didn't end there. I got a terrific radio job in San Diego and was also asked by a major publisher to write a funny memoir. Of course I named it Not Skinny, Not Blonde. *I also filmed a successful Showtime special, "The Latin Divas of Comedy," which was nominated for an Alma award.*

Monique's Relationship with Comedy

The best analogy I can offer is that comedy gave to me what most people hope a child will do for them. Comedy is my child. You have to love something more than yourself, something more than your human body and your human frailties. Something has to make you want to be bigger than you are. I love comedy so much, the power of making people laugh. There's nothing I wouldn't do for comedy. Comedy gives my life meaning because there's something about the way I communicate that alleviates people's worries. I feel I was marked for something—it's my purpose. I have no ego; I am very grateful. Comedy is my purest place, and I would do it for nothing, and have.

I've got to say, though, that it's been a long and hard ride, making this life in comedy work. Comedy humbled me. I slept on couches of strangers, I never said no to a gig. Comedy rocked me to my foundation, and there was nothing I wouldn't do to keep doing it, to keep it alive, to keep it thriving and healthy. I've been in car wrecks, been blown off the road in a blizzard, run out of gas in the middle of the night. But it's always come out all right. I believe the universe conspires to protect you and move you forward when you're on the path you're meant to be on.

Monique shows us that following your talents and gifts doesn't mean life will be easy. Far from it. We're often tested on this path to develop the "chops" of remaining steadfast and strong in our belief in ourselves, despite what the "three-dimensional world," as Monique puts it, is showing us in the moment. As anyone who has pursued a nontraditional path knows, when you go against the grain, against what the majority sees as the right or sensible type of life to live, you will face challenge, adversity, and ridicule. But if you feel about your profession and gifts the way Monique feels about hers, you will do almost anything to nurture them. This type of calling inspires you to move mountains to follow it.

My husband, Arthur Lipner, has this type of calling as a musician, composer, and performer. Like Monique, Arthur has found that living the life of an artist today can be grueling, gut-wrenching, and can knock you to your knees. But he couldn't walk away even if he wanted to. Music is who he is in his bones, what he came here to do and share, and the legacy he will leave to others. I too feel that I will never turn my back on myself again. I will stick this out—following my talents as an author, coach, and speaker—because I feel it's what I'm meant to do. And because I love it.

Even if you don't feel this type of calling, your life is much richer when you commit to doing what you love, in some form or another. When you accept what you are gifted at and love doing, and dedicate yourself to bringing your gifts forward in life and work, your life experience takes on a completely new and powerful dimension. Then you are living for something greater than yourself, something deeper, more connected, and supremely beneficial in the world.

Challenge is inevitable in human experience. So why not experience it while living a life you find joyful and purposeful? Find new ways to use your natural talents. When you do, you'll be serving your highest good and the greater good of others.

Monique says of her life now: *My life is beyond my wildest dreams now. I love comedy with all my heart and always have, but now I'm able to do it in ways that are far bigger and more exciting than I could have hoped. I say that I'm "angel retentive" now—I've been blessed with so many people who are angels in my life, who support me and move me forward. I feel like my gift and my purpose is comedy, that's what I am here for. I can thank my many angels and the universe for conspiring to help and protect me all along the way. Comedy is like my child. I keep going, believing in myself and in comedy, even through the tough times. After all, would you give up your child after five years just because they're not turning out as you hoped?*

There are several key lessons in Monique's story. The first is that each and every one of us is special and important in the world. We are each born with beautiful, much-needed talents and abilities. If we don't use and develop them in this lifetime, who will? These abilities have coalesced uniquely through your distinct life experiences, perceptions, tribulations, and triumphs. They are not random, and they should not be squandered or thrown aside.

The second vital lesson we learn from Monique is that nothing ensures your sense of joy and purpose more than drawing on those very gifts that make you *you*. The capabilities that you love to draw upon are those you're meant to use. Doing so to earn your living—if you can—brings great reward and fulfillment. It's not a lark or a whim to want to earn your living doing what you love. Sometimes we can find ways to use these talents for our sole livelihood, and sometimes not. If not, it's vital to bring them forward in other ways. And sometimes you have to do other work for a while, as Amanda did, to pay your bills while you're finding your legs in your new line of work. But completely turning your back on your longings is wasting precious time. Your gifts connect you to a higher purpose. Your gifts allow you to be of joyful service to others.

MONIQUE'S ADVICE

- Figure out what natural talents and gifts you have, and decide which ones you can't live without expressing. Devote yourself to these special gifts, as if they're your children.
- Believe without a doubt that you can follow your path, no matter what others say. Let go of the fear that you can't do it.
- Recognize and be open to the angels in your life. Open your heart to those who are available, ready, and more than willing to help when you get clear on your path.

Know Your Natural Talents

Do you know what your special talents and gifts are? I'm referring to those natural, innate capabilities that emerged in childhood and have been with you all along, *and you love to use them*. Some of your skills may not bring you joy. I happen to be good at giving presentations to a board room of senior executives, complete with P&L's and financial forecasts, but I hate doing it—it bores me to tears. If certain skills feel boring or meaningless to you, then developing a career around them makes very little sense.

Using the natural talents you *love*—the ones that make you feel special and important when you share them with others—brings a feeling of connectedness and useful-ness in the world. Whether or not you've developed these talents, they are still inside of you. For instance, I've always been a good singer. I sang a great deal in my twenties but turned away from performing once I had children and a demanding career, due to my perceived lack of time. Ten years later, when I realized that my life is simply much hap-pier when I'm singing, I committed myself to performing regularly, working the craft, and sharing it with others. I adore singing, whether it's in groups, with my husband, or solo. I can't and won't live without it now. Interestingly, when you get committed to using gifts and talents and decide to bring them forward, opportunities appear that encourage you to do so.

The first step in connecting deeply with your gifts and talents is to identify the spe-cial abilities you possessed in childhood that were easy, enjoyable, exciting to use, and that others took notice of and praised. How have you been helpful to others while ex-pressing your very essence? Below is a list of special talents and gifts that people possess and love to use. Which of these represent your distinctive gifts?

Acting	Decorating
Adapting	Demonstrating
Administrating	Designing
Assisting	Developing
Building	Directing
Challenging	Drawing
Changing	Elaborating
Cleaning	Enacting
Composing	Entertaining
Conducting	Envisioning
Consoling	Expressing
Constructing	Figuring
Conveying	Formulating
Cooking	Giving
Correcting	Guiding
Creating	Healing
Dancing	Illustrating

Improvising	Planning
Inspiring	Preparing
Inventing	Presenting
Invigorating	Producing
Laughing	Restoring
Leading	Restructuring
Loving	Shaping
Making	Sharing
Managing	Singing
Motivating	Speaking
Nurturing	Teaching
Observing	Telling
Orchestrating	Testing
Ordering	Validating
Painting	Writing
Performing	Other _____

Wanting to express your special, unique gifts is not whimsical. It is essential. The more you express your distinctive combination of talents, the more able you are to create a satisfying and meaningful life. And in doing so, you change your world for the better.

Get Solid in Your Belief in Yourself

Monique's story reveals another critical point. Doing what you love does not guarantee that the money will follow. Once Monique did the inner and outer work of aligning herself unwaveringly with her calling, money started to flow. This takes time (much longer than we'd like, sometimes) and action. Monique followed her gift of comedy but in the beginning went through hell and back to do so. Monique eventually learned that a secure, stable, and joyful life requires having an unshakable belief in yourself and your actions. Don't give in to self-doubt. Ignore the naysayers and critical judges. Misgivings, doubts, and fears about what you're doing will be reflected in your actions and your life experience.

At first you will be fearful and insecure when you step up to using your talents. Such feelings are inevitable. Why? Because these gifts mean everything to you. They are why you are here. To risk failure, embarrassment, and incompetence in the arena of your core talents is intimidating because these gifts represent the "real" you. No one wants to be less than fabulous when their authentic self is at stake. But when you move forward in spite of your fears and insecurities, you give yourself more and more evidence that you are truly terrific at utilizing these talents—or you have the capacity to be. You and your abilities matter in the world! Sure, you may need some work—perhaps even a little help—at sharing your talents and figuring out exactly how to apply them. But the fact remains, these are your gifts and always will be.

To follow this path of honoring and utilizing your talents, hold a steadfast belief in the rightness of doing so. Believe completely in the importance of who you are, and of sharing your unique essence. Others will try to knock you off this path—that's a given—because what you're doing intimidates them. Many people are stuck in slavehood to their fears, and they want you to be stuck with them. But if you want to remain motivated, ask yourself, "Can I stay committed to this path that feels good and true to me, despite what others say?" As you get better at moving forward unflinchingly, and feeling good about it despite what the world presents to you in the moment, then you will find a way to make it. And others will come to your assistance when you need it most.

Be Open to Angels in Your Life

Finally, Monique's story reveals the importance of other people in our lives who believe in and support us unconditionally. These mentors, supporters, and facilitators trust in us completely. They see the stunning future version of us, even though we have not yet stepped up to create it. These individuals are nothing short of angels. They love us, nurture us, hold us to higher standards, comfort us in tough times, and offer us the "gentle fire" (as my friend Mike Jaffe calls it) we need to push forward into the unknown. They have far greater insight and foresight than we do because we're steeped in fear that we'll fail and they are not. Angels act on their great insight in powerful and loving ways.

Monique's angels are many—from Dixie, the generous woman who hired her anytime she was passing through, to Jeffrey, Monique's brilliant manager who sought her out and believed in her amazing capabilities before they were fully realized. My angels have been many as well, including my husband, who supports me in all my new wild directions, despite how illogical they may appear, and my mother, who has always said to me, "I know you can do whatever you want to in life—just do it!"

Angels come to us all the time, ready and able to help. But to act on their help and to move yourself forward, and to attract more angels who support you, requires believing powerfully and resolutely in yourself. In Monique's wise words, "Be angel-retentive!" When you are, your angels will help you move mountains.

MOVING FORWARD TO BREAKTHROUGH

✷ STEP BACK

In your journal, capture all your thoughts. *No censoring, please—write everything that comes to mind.*

- What have I been gifted at and talented in since my childhood?
- What do my friends and family say are my gifts and talents? (Ask them!)
- When I have used my talents previously, how did it go? What felt best about it? What was scary about it?
- Looking over my whole life and career, what are all the things that I'm great at *and* love to do?
- In my current situation, am I using these talents? If not, am I ready to explore directions where I could?

✷ LET GO of your fears of failure and inadequacy.

Think about what you are most afraid of when it comes to using your talents. Explore this fear. Get to know it very well.

- What does it look and feel like?
- When have you had this fear?
- What brings it on? How often do you have it?
- What coping skills have you acquired to push forward through this fear?

- What small step can you take this month to push through your fear of failure, and bring your talent forward? (For example, seek a career coach, take a lesson, make a call to a potential mentor in the field, do research, or enroll in a class.)

If you're still reluctant, find support from one of your "angels" to help you. Who will you contact this month for support?

✳ **SAY YES!** to believing in your talents without fail.

Visualize your powerful "Future Self" using your natural gifts and talents, sharing them with the world, and loving doing so.

Visualizing Your Gifted Future Self

Find a comfortable spot to sit, relaxed and uninterrupted. Close your eyes. Take three long, deep breaths, relaxing more deeply with each breath.

In your mind's eye, picture in detail your Future Self, years from now. Watch as your Future Self moves through life and work, beautiful, confident, joyful, and powerful, using the talents that most compel you. Observe this Future Self in many different situations, both in your work and in your family life.

See your Future Self working with others, doing what you do best, and loving it. Others enjoy who you are, and the benefits of your talents unfold. People praise you, applaud you, shake your hand, and thank you for what you've given them. You have helped them, and they express their deep gratitude.

Feel the joy that your Future Self experiences, and watch beautiful images of your strength and confidence. See clearly how the world is richer because you are in it.

When you are ready to speak to your Future Self, see her embracing the current you. She loves and respects you very much. She whispers something very important in your ear, something she knows will help you accept your talents and move forward to use them. She is wise and all-knowing, and you trust her.

You thank her, and she says good-bye, showing you out the door. See the current you smiling, more confident and self-assured, with a new bounce in your step. You know that she has helped you on your way.

- From this visualization, what did you learn about

  - The talents and gifts you wish to bring forward?
  - The shifts in your life and work you can make today that will allow you to utilize your gifts and talents more fully?
  - How your talents are of benefit to others, and the world?

- What did your Future Self whisper in your ear?
- What one step can you take this month to honor your gifts and talents more fully, in life and work?

Remember

You are here to make full use of your unique talents, and to do so joyfully. Anything less is wasting time. You are not a random occurrence but a special, essential combination of everything you are and everything you've experienced. Move ahead honoring your gifts, even in the face of your fears. You will be thankful you did.

Monique reminds us

"Follow the thing that you love more than yourself, the thing that makes you more than your human body and your human frailties. Something has to make you want you to be bigger than you are. Find out what that is, what you were marked for, let go of your fears, your worries, and your ego, and just do it. Angels will come to help you."

✳ **BREAKTHROUGH** "I use my real talents in life and work."

12

Helping Others and the World

I get up every morning determined both to change the world and to have one hell of a good time. Sometimes, this makes planning the day difficult.

E. B. WHITE

EMPOWERMENT WITH THE WORLD

✳ **STEP BACK TO EXPLORE** Resisting the fact that you can make a difference.

✳ **LET GO** of believing you don't have what it takes.

✳ **SAY YES!** to changing the world.

✳ **BREAKTHROUGH**
"I help others and the world."

✳ **Laurie:** *I suppose you could call my professional experience of several years ago a "crisis," but truthfully, I've been through such personal traumas that I don't use the word lightly. I'm a mother of two, Luke (16 years old now) and Dylan (14), who are the loves of my life, along with my husband, Grayle. Luke is a surviving twin, and we lost our son Jason at 6 days old. That was a true medical and personal crisis, and it was unspeakably painful. My newborn babies were terribly ill, and Luke survived with significant special needs. After that experience, everything pales in comparison. This life experience, of losing Jason, and now having two precious children—one of whom has extensive special needs—has given me so much that is a blessing, and I've received real perspective from it.*

About my professional life . . . I started out in education. I was a first-grade and special-education teacher. That was the path I thought I'd take for my entire career. I believed I'd be principal of an elementary school, or start my own school someday. Candidly, my life and career changed directions because my boyfriend at the time dumped me. I was devastated, and knew I needed a change, so I decided to move my life back to New York. I then found my way into the world of publishing. I started on the sales side, then moved onto marketing and finally into management. I eventually joined Time Inc., in New York City, where I stayed for seven years until I left in December 2005.

In the initial years, I really enjoyed the whole experience of that career path. I felt I was learning something new every day, and the industry was fun. I was going through a real ascension, and it was exciting because I believed I was making a difference and a contribution. After selling for a variety of publications, I became the director of a large sales group. Most recently I was at Fortune *magazine, as the marketing director. After several years, they made me a VP, and I took on lots of interesting and varied responsibilities. I traveled*

✳ Laurie Howlett is a 53-year-old former Vice President of Marketing, *Fortune* Magazine Group; currently she is a special-needs advocate and author of a special-needs children's book series.

149

as far up the ladder as I wanted to go and was really excited because I had "made it," but I had done so on my terms, or so I thought.

Laurie's story holds an important message. If we were able to chart all of the events in our lives from a higher perspective, as an outside observer, we'd see that we are being prepared for a purpose that isn't readily apparent to us in the moment. We'd see that each of us is special, needed, important. If we follow what we love and what feels good—our authentic path—no matter how challenging it may seem, it will lead us to where we dream of going.

Laurie continues: *As a mother of two, with a son who had special needs, I created a flexible schedule where I worked from home on Fridays. I felt good about that . . . I was the only manager to do so, and they agreed to the terms that I needed. In the world of* Fortune *magazine, I was one of the lone women . . . the first working mom in the executive committee. Along with a colleague I launched a very successful women's conference, which was a powerful event and proved very beneficial to women. So it felt great to be in a man's world, but as a woman with a very strong voice.*

In the beginning, I know I surprised people—pleasantly, I think—particularly the men, and I found the work to be stimulating and enjoyable. At times, I had the sense that my male colleagues weren't quite sure what to do with me, and often there was much posturing and pontificating. Frankly, at times I had to regard my male counterparts as if they were obstreperous clients; in which case, you have to figure out how to connect with them so they can hear you and you can hear them, in order to accomplish the business at hand.

As the first working mother on the executive committee, I shook things up, helping people get more connected with what they valued, and I found meaning in that. But over time, something shifted and I began to move away from enjoying "playing with the boys." Don't get me wrong. There were certainly some women I couldn't work with. And I found it all really fatiguing, navigating through the lack of heart and emotional disconnection, and the competitive posturing. I was doing very well; that wasn't the issue. It was a question of where I wanted to put my energies, and how I wanted to make a difference. After all I'd given at work to build my career to where I wanted it, there were days I'd wake up anxious, worried, and questioning, "Is this all there is?" I'd think about my son Luke. His needs are great—he doesn't talk, the only word he says is "Mom" (though I think that makes him fluent, so I don't have a problem with that!). He was in a real school crisis for a couple of years, and in serious distress. I got him through that, and I kept thinking to myself, "There's no more important job than this, than being a mom. There must be something else I can be do-ing, something more significant, to make this world a better place, for him, for children, for others." I began to yearn deeply to make a change and a difference in the world in a much bigger way than I had access to, but I just didn't know how to in my current situation.

Laurie felt at ease being one of the boys, and her big personality—her outgoing de-meanor and confidence, talent, forthrightness, and humor—helped her achieve success in the corporate world. At first, she was accepted and highly admired for her strength and her points of difference among her male coworkers. It was all going beautifully. Her work seemed to be a good fit, until something changed. A yearning emerged, slowly and steadily, to apply her energies to something bigger, something more meaningful to her, something more influential to the world at large.

Laurie continues: *Several years went by in which I was truly restless, yearning, and didn't know which direction to go. I was in a limbo that stretched me in completely different directions, and I couldn't resolve which one to take. I tried some different things during those years to fill my heart, but those experiences led me to feel even more restless at work. Then, dealing with all the male energy just lost its appeal completely. I realized that I was spending too much energy on trying to change this corporate environment, breaking myself against it. I asked myself, "Why do I care so much about this?" I didn't have aspirations to become a publisher, so I'd gone as far as I wanted to go there. And further, I wasn't willing to sacrifice my heart in the process of being successful, and it was looking like the fight to keep my heart alive was requiring me to give up my soul. The men were just too uncomfortable.*

Over time, the fatigue wore me down. I was tired, depressed, and worn out. I'd ask my sister, with whom I'm very close and who was also in the corporate world, "How did we get here?" And then the economy took a major downturn and it affected the organization terri-bly. When business turns difficult in tough economic times, some wonky behavior in people gets exposed because they don't know how to fix it. Instead of approaching the new economy with a collaborative spirit, it became very much cutthroat and a cruel, blaming world.

So, in 2003, I decided I had to find a way out, and leave, but I didn't know where to go next. I was scared about it . . . walking away from what I'd created, leaving without a safety net. I'd worked so hard for what I'd achieved. At this point, the company was going through murmurings of staff reductions. At the same time, I met a great woman who ran a com-munications company in Connecticut, and she offered me a job. The commute was shorter, but the compensation wasn't what I hoped it would be, and also I'd have to report to a man who was doing a job I could've done. I knew if I were to take another corporate job, it would have to be as a direct report to the top. The whole experience helped me realize that I indeed did want to leave Fortune, but I no longer wanted to work in the corporate world. I was done.

My husband and I discussed all this, and we agreed to start planning for me to make a significant change. For two years I had been working on a book about my special-needs son, and I realized that this might be the time and place to begin focus on writing my book, and turn my heart toward the community of special-needs kids that I was so devoted to and loved. I said to my husband, "Not everyone has a capacity to work with these kids or to be a voice for this community, and is there any better cause than Luke?" I realized then that finishing the book—which I saw as a catalyst to create a platform for the special-needs community—was the direction that would tie my whole life together.

As luck would have it, in November 2003, through the rumblings of layoffs and packages, I decided to let fate take its course, rather than endeavoring to push a direction for myself. Thankfully, they offered me a package, and I took it. It had taken me years in the corporate world to figure out who I was and what I truly wanted, from the heart. There was a core of myself that I was in touch with, but parts of me hadn't been fully realized or expressed. I decided to take the leap and jump, without a net, into a world that finally answered the longings of my heart and soul.

After Laurie's Leap

After twenty years in the corporate world, this has been a great opportunity to stop, relax, unwind, take a nap, or go lie in the hammock because I can. At first it took me a while to orient myself, but I was really ready. Keep in mind, my children had two parents who commuted into the city and were both in New York City during 9/11. In these times in the world when anything can happen, I decided I needed and wanted to be here for my kids more.

About my book on Luke, my writing process initially was that I'd think about a special moment in Luke's life and write it. A friend of mine called it "puking out the story." After puking out a tremendous amount, I needed to put structure around it. I started meeting and talking with many other moms of special-needs kids, and I discovered that, while we vary in the details of our situations, we are all connected in the feelings and the journey— these are very universal. I've found that other moms love this book and idea, and they tell me it's an incredible, inspiring story. I know I have to write this . . . I'm connected in my heart and soul to it.

And then one day I concluded that I'd written everything that I needed and wanted to say (for the moment), and I wasn't sure in which direction I would take it. So I decided that, instead of pushing this, I would turn my energy inward and take time for me to rediscover "me." My decision happened to coincide with summer vacation for my younger son, Dylan, and we agreed that we'd play together during his break.

As always happens in my life, because I was completely connected to my heart during this time, my idea for my Lambdoodle children's book series was born. I came to it so easily and realized that it was there all along, but to see it required a full "detox" from my formerly overscheduled, exhausting life. As of this moment, my book series proposal is now complete. I've met with many publishing and media contacts, all of whom have been enthusiastically supportive of my endeavor, which has also led to a new business that is separate from the multimedia platform.

I talk to everyone about my book now. Today, one in five families has a special-needs child, yet it's still a profoundly underserved community—a forgotten community in our world of many experts who are often incompetent and uncaring. It is very easy for others who don't understand to stuff special-needs kids into programs that most often are barely adequate, leaving one to wonder if the rest of the world either doesn't care or is unaware. People say, "Okay, fine, put the child there, he'll be happy. He has special needs, so it's okay. He doesn't have to be as productive as other people." But this couldn't be farther from the truth. My dream is to be an ambassador for the special-needs community, because this community desperately needs attention and service, and I can help.

The ultimate goal for my project is to create a huge and powerful platform for special-needs families—complete with support groups for families, extensive resource connections, and an inspiring children's book series (now called Lambdoodle) whose shining heroes are special-needs kids. My work also underscores the special attributes of the wonderful school Luke is in now that took us years to find. I'd like to use it as a model to start other schools. There are shockingly few quality schools and services for special-needs children and young adults today, and I plan to do something about that.

About money—it's a necessity, of course, and it's important to me to be able to make a good living, and be financially independent. I'm still working through the financial reality, and the fear of the unknown sometimes surfaces. I continue to revere my financial independence, but I trust that my next journey will provide me adequate compensation. I'm not sure how it will happen, but I trust that it will. Relinquishing my salary and letting my husband support us solely for a while was a very big step for me. But I know I have strong talents and an important project that will translate to compensation. I'm not overcome with financial worries. I just trust.

Laurie says of her life now: *I've been through deep traumas. Every day I wake up and my life is punctuated with perspective. I go to sleep with perspective. I have learned to relax into life. I don't doubt for a moment my intent to transform the world of special needs, or the profound difference that I can make for special-needs kids, their families, and others who are connected to those with special needs. I have trusted for some time that this is my heartfelt path—my destiny. I am committed to being present, and savoring the preciousness of every minute of my life if I can. My life journey has shown me the importance of loving and accepting it all as a gift.*

LAURIE'S ADVICE

- Walk away from the fear or resistance of forging an authentic path.
- Enjoy the preciousness of life.
- Trust that you can help the world. Do not doubt for a moment that you can transform it for the better.

Stop Resisting Your New Path

For many women, fear and resistance become abundant when they think about doing something powerful, different, bold, or untraditional. I've met many women who have the inkling that they can indeed help the world, but they snuff it out quickly, doubting that this longing could ever come to fruition or that they are "big" enough to make it happen. Laurie had been working on her book for two years and had desired for even longer to help special-needs children. Thankfully, she said yes! to these longings when the opportunity presented itself to dedicate herself to them. Taking the plunge toward embracing a new path, if it's something you feel you can't live without, is a vital step.

What is behind women's reluctance to say yes! to themselves? Were we raised with an overly accommodating worldview? Was it ingrained that women should put others ahead of themselves? Or perhaps it's simply a comfortable and believable excuse to say that something outside of ourselves is holding us back. Whatever the reasons, women find it difficult to operate on their own instructions, on their own behalf, and move toward powerful action, especially if others are skeptical or less than accepting.

Laurie says: *What I discovered is that it requires a great deal of confidence and courage to travel the unknown path, and move away from what others say and think. It's very challenging, too, not having all of the answers or knowing exactly how it will all turn out in the face of the constant questions from others: for example, what are you working on, how is it going, when will it be published, etc. My spiritual journey is a constant in my life. And my daily practice allows me to connect to my heart, and to a source that is meaningful to me. I've become quite comfortable now with the fact that I've been working on my idea for about eighteen months and still don't know the exact details of how this will come to fruition but continue to trust that it will. I've let go of my linear thinking and thrown out any timetable that I may have once placed on myself.*

I was more affected by "tribal thinking" in my past (the thoughts and opinions of the majority group in which I lived or worked—whether it was religious thought, or male behaviors and views, or corporate dictates). But frankly, I don't focus often on these types of dominant thoughts and opinions anymore. I am devoted to living my own life, not theirs.

Laurie has found that her connection with her spirituality gives her the strength to persist in her own meaningful endeavors and tune out the chatter of those who would question, criticize, or judge. Finding what you need to help you move through fear and resistance is critical, so that you can step up to what you dream of being and doing. Whether it's changing the world to better serve the special-needs community, writing a book, cherishing your family time, or moving from a heart-deprived working world to a heart-filled one, understand what you long for most. Push forward to it, despite your fear and resistance.

Enjoy Life's Preciousness

Writing this chapter on Laurie's life has changed me, given me deeper perspective, altered how I view the little nothings that perturb my sense of calm and balance. I'm not sure how long this new perspective will last (forever, I hope), but I feel that I'm looking through different glasses now—ones that block out the trivial and help me see more clearly what is vitally important in living fully.

Imagine what we could be and create if we could let go of the trivial, meaningless stuff that clutters our minds and lives—the irritating boss, the jealous friend, the critical behavior of our siblings, the haughty neighbor—and dedicated ourselves to feeling completely alive and relishing the preciousness of every moment. This commitment to embracing the preciousness of life alters our experience dramatically. Losing a child and having a special-needs son has given Laurie perspective like no other life events could. And it shows. She lives every day from a worldview that nothing matters more than loving your life, cherishing the heart connection and time you have with your special loved ones, and devoting yourself unabashedly to your visions of serving as an agent of change in the world.

Trust That You Can Help the World

If you long to help others and the world, then you are *supposed to be helping the world.* It's that simple. You wouldn't be fantasizing about it, yearning for it if you weren't capable of it. You resonate with something outside yourself only if it is already a part of you, something that exists inside you, wanting and needing expression. So many women do not act on their longings. Not acting on your desires to help others or the world simply means you are frittering away your precious chance to make a difference.

What do you long to do that is in service to others and the world? If it's a very large endeavor, great! Take small, bite-sized steps toward it—break it down into manageable actions that give you evidence you're capable of being the person you dream of being. If your way of helping the world doesn't fit your current situation, it's up to you to somehow incorporate your vision of helping so that it does.

You are capable of stepping up to help the world. You wouldn't be reading these words if you weren't. Trust me on this one. Your destiny is waiting for you to claim it.

MOVING FORWARD TO BREAKTHROUGH

✳ STEP BACK

Visualization: Remembering When You Made a Difference

Close your eyes, and take three long, deep breaths.

Think back over your life. Bring to your mind's eye a very important event that made a lasting positive impression on you, a time when you were of great help to someone. Go back as far as you'd like, even to your teen years or childhood.

See the moment clearly. Watch how you stepped forward to help. Who did you help? What did you do specifically? Observe how you made them feel better, gave them support and assistance when they needed it most. See how you took care of them when no one else did. See the strength, courage, and compassion you shared.

How did they respond when you offered your help? How did *you* feel? Feel it now.

You'll remember this moment for a long time, and most likely so will they. Why was it so memorable? Because you changed the world—their world and yours—just for a moment.

Whenever you think you can't change the world, remember this moment. Making a difference in the world is simple—it's doing what you did. It's stepping forward to help in any way you can that feels right. That's all it takes.

✳ LET GO of believing you don't have what it takes.

What do you think it takes to change the world? Is it tremendous ability, money, time? Or can we change the world with small steps, one at a time?

- Write down the many skills and talents you've developed over your lifetime that could be useful in your vision of helping the world. Include skills you love to use from all your jobs, volunteer work, parenting experience, hobbies . . . everything that makes you *you* that you love to do. Your list might include marketing, writing, leading, organizing, networking, researching, fund-raising, planning, public speaking, entertaining, teaching, or financial forecasting.
- Now write your bio with this full list of talents and skills. Read it over. See, you have what it takes!

✳ SAY YES! to changing the world.

Below is a list of ways people help the world. Review the list, and check off any category that appeals to you. Also write down specific areas that compel you (special-needs children, the environment, hospice, etc.).

Ways to Help the World[1]	*Specific Areas I'm Attracted to*
___ Assisting in Creating Results	_____
___ Counseling/Coaching People	_____
___ Supporting/Assisting Children	_____
___ Supporting the Elderly	_____
___ Enhancing Health and Wellness Issues	_____
___ Supporting Political, Environmental, or Social Causes	_____
___ Bringing Creativity to Life	_____
___ Helping Family and Friends	_____
___ Increasing Others' Quality of Life	_____
___ Providing Quality Services/Products	_____
___ Enhancing Beauty	_____
___ Training Others	_____
___ Teaching Others	_____
___ Enhancing Fun for Others	_____
___ Supporting Others' Organizational Capability	_____
___ Streamlining Processes and Organizations	_____
___ Creating New Businesses/Projects/Events	_____

Other ways to make a difference:

_____   _____

_____   _____

- Of the categories above, choose the top three helping areas that most strongly compel you, and list them in order of importance to you (1 = most important).

    1. _____

    2. _____

    3. _____

- Take action this month to explore these areas: research them online, talk to people who do this work, call an organization, or take a class.

Your Vision of Helping

In reviewing Laurie's story, we can see she had the following ingredients that helped her vision become a reality:

HEARTFELT CONNECTION	To her special-needs child, who needed her
HER VISION	To help special-needs children gain self-reliance and live empowered, joyful lives
ABILITY TO COMMIT	Room in her heart and her life to contribute with time and energy
TALENTS/SKILLS	Writing, networking, executing plans, marketing

Uncover your unique vision for helping the world, and realize all the abilities and talents you have developed over your lifetime that will help. Complete this chart today:

My Vision for Helping the World

MY HEARTFELT CONNECTION IS TO:	
MY VISION:	
HOW I CAN COMMIT:	
MY TALENTS I CAN USE:	
MY NEXT STEP:	

Your vision is waiting to be created. Don't wait. Go for it!

Remember

If you long to help the world, then you are *supposed to be helping others and the world.* Being who you are makes a difference. Don't doubt it for a second longer. Take action today to push through your fear and resistance.

Laurie reminds us

"I've practiced celebrating each and every contact I make—no matter where it leads. My belief is that when one door closes, multiple new ones open and you have no idea where those will take you . . . and hooray for that! I find that the more I speak out loud about what I'm committed to, the more it takes shape, the more I own it, and the further I empower myself and my concept of helping the world."

✳ **BREAKTHROUGH** "I help others and the world."

EMPOWERMENT WITH HIGHER SELF

13

Falling Together
After Falling Apart

*Everything can be taken from a man but
one thing; the last of the human freedoms—
to choose one's attitude in any given set of
circumstances, to choose one's own way.*

VIKTOR FRANKL
Man's Search for Meaning

EMPOWERMENT WITH HIGHER SELF

✳ **Theresa:** *Truthfully, I don't talk much about my background and childhood because people just get overwhelmed about it, feel sorry for me, or see only the difficulties. But I really don't view it that way. I believe that everything that's happened to me has made me who I am, and I wouldn't change any of it. The reality is that I was born to a mother who was imprisoned for being a con artist, and as a baby I was handed off to my mother's sister. I suffered abuse in her home and was removed by the state. I was taken in by a series of foster homes for the next several years and was placed in my final adoptive home when I was 6. It was a small farm in Kansas, and I had a very modest upbringing. I worked all the time, and there was no TV, no playtime, no frills, nothing was wasted. Basically, if we didn't grow it or kill it, we didn't eat it. We were very poor, and certain days of the week we would have to go to the trash dumpster behind the grocery store to get our vegetables to eat.*

Growing up, I had two very powerful role models—my adopted mother and grandmother. Both were very strong, resourceful women. To my mother, there was nothing that couldn't be accomplished. Despite all that she was going through, I never heard her once complain or say, "Why is this happening to me?" She did what had to be done and worked from sun up to sun down. I learned so much from her. It's funny, I tell my kids now, "I can rebuild your engine, change your oil, and milk a cow, but don't ask me to do the Martha Stewart stuff." My childhood was all about being resourceful, doing what had to be done, and wasting nothing. We were disciplined, always working.

I was lucky that I did experience love from my mother. She was as loving as she could be, given the fact that my adoptive father was terribly abusive to all of us. He spent time in prison for his abuse, and after prison, he committed suicide in a violent way. He set the house on fire and then shot himself to death. Even through that, my mother kept going, try-

---

✳ Theresa Wilson, 40, formerly a TV journalist, is the founder of The Blessing Basket Project®.[1]   163 *ing to be there for her five adopted children as best she could. She didn't always succeed, but she did her best to be there for us.*

Theresa's childhood story is full of suffering, trauma, and hardship. But when you speak with her, sadness and pain are not the feelings that emerge. What you hear is courage, confidence, resilience, and hope. From all that she endured, she has become strong, independent—in short, a survivor. She refuses to be a victim of her past. Instead, she chooses to use all that she's suffered to rise above her current situation and be a powerful vehicle for change. Her mother and her grandmother provided two courageous role models for fortitude and endurance. She witnessed firsthand every day what's required to keep going in life despite crushing challenges. Theresa saw her mother and grandmother rise above their trials, showing an unshakable commitment to putting one foot in front of the other and being the best they could be for those who needed them.

Theresa's Adult Crisis

In 1999, I had a deep personal crisis. Out of the blue, my husband of thirteen years simply walked out on me and our two children, who were 5 and 7 at the time. It was Valentine's Day, and I remember he gave me two dozen roses in the morning, and by nighttime, he had left us, walked out, gone forever. I was absolutely shattered. I truly didn't see it coming.

I had a job as a TV journalist, but my salary wasn't nearly enough to take care of all our bills. For months I struggled, trying to earn enough money, be there for my kids, and hold things together, but everything was falling apart. It really did feel like a sort of death. Here was a person I loved and thought I'd be with for the rest of my life, who just bailed on us with no warning whatsoever. It was a horrific experience, and I went through a long period of great turmoil. I didn't really come to until about a year and half later when I began to feel stronger and get the sense that I'd be okay. And with each passing year I felt stronger and stronger. But the key symptom for me during this time was that every problem, no matter how big or how small, from bald tires needing repair to my children crying, everything seemed so magnified, so larger than life. It was like, "I can't bear this, too!" I couldn't tolerate the crabby boss, the whining child who needed a nap. I just felt so overwhelmed by the simplest thing. I felt like, "I can't take one more thing here." Everything felt like too much.

As hard as it was, I realize now that this period, this traumatic experience, represents the seed for The Blessing Basket Project®.

Theresa's crisis of "everything falling apart" is typical—an enormous event occurs that shifts everything all at once. In this crisis experience, something you view as cataclysmic transpires so that nothing looks or feels the same as it once did. This shift, while deeply unsettling, can bring into focus the most important elements of who you are if you let it. It allows you to see more clearly what to let go of in order to move forward. This shift also brings into clearer view what you wish to be and do in this lifetime.

The Blessing Basket Project Is Born

During my period of crisis, people around me started sending me cards and letters of encouragement and support. I'd lay them out on the mantel and look at them frequently. Then one day, I collected them all and put them in a basket that one of these kind individuals had given me. It was a beautiful split-wood basket, and I started calling it my "blessing basket" because it was a place I kept all of these wonderful blessings from others. Other items began to find their way in there, too, like a piece of old tire from the time I couldn't afford to buy new tires for my car, and I had decided to cash in my life insurance policy for the money. That day, a colleague at my office who knew what I was going through asked me, "Have you cashed in your policy yet?" I said, "Not yet. I'm going to do it tonight." Then he handed me his credit card and said, "Don't do it, Theresa. Go buy some tires and take care of anything else you need." The kindness and generosity I've received from people, many of whom were strangers, still awe me. There was another time I simply couldn't pay my monthly bills, and I got a phone call from a woman who said, "Hi, Theresa. My name is Ruth. You don't know me, but I've been instructed to take care of your electric bill this month."

These words and acts of kindness and love kept pouring in. At night, after a particularly hard day when the kids were in bed, I'd sit there with a cup of tea, desperately trying to figure how I'd get through another day, financially, emotionally—being a mother, a professional, taking care of all these responsibilities. I'd glance over and there'd be my blessing basket. I'd pore through it, reading the words of encouragement. I'd think, "Maria's praying for me," or "So-and-so gave me these groceries. I've got to go on. They've made an investment in me." My basket kept me going. My crisis then reminded me of my mother's experience when my father was sent to prison. I thought to myself, "I've got to survive this for the sake of my children," just as my mother must have said about us.

As I started to feel stronger, I began teaching women's groups about overcoming struggle and trauma, and how to survive it. In leading these workshops, I discussed my special blessing basket and what it did for me. Women all over found this concept very powerful and wanted to buy a basket for themselves. So I acquired some baskets from a neat woman in Arizona who imported them. As I sold them, I heard amazing stories about how these baskets helped women heal and survive their challenges. One woman came up to me and said,

"My blessing basket got me through the death of my husband." Another said, "I found a way to pay my bills thanks to this basket," and so on. It was clear that this concept—gathering remembrances of one's blessings in one spot and being reminded of the love and support that surrounds us—was changing people's lives. I loved this idea but was bothered that the baskets I sold simply said "Made in China." I realized I wanted to know who the individual maker was, and to bless the maker of the basket as well as the recipient.

As time went on, I realized too that I wanted to do something to help the world in a big way. My dream was to reduce world poverty. I was discussing my dream with a friend, and she said, "So, what's stopping you?" What a powerful question that proved to be. I decided from that moment on that I needed to stop making excuses and do something. I asked her to help me be accountable, to stop making excuses for myself, and to take action, and she did just that.

It is a deep passion of mine to do something meaningful to reduce poverty, I think because I grew up very poor and I'm deeply compassionate about the needs of the impoverished. This is an issue I am very concerned about, an issue close to my heart. So I moved forward with my dream and did something.

For eight months, I underwent a whole education process on how to sell beautiful hand-woven baskets from third world countries and bless the makers of these baskets by paying the highest wages possible for their services. I first found a missionary in Bangladesh who helped me get her baskets out, in the summer of 2003. They sold, and sold quickly. I became very excited and said to myself, "I think I can pull this off!" I sold the baskets everywhere I could, at local fairs and festivals in the St. Louis area, and through word of mouth. Then when November 2003 rolled around, I got remarried to a wonderful man, Bryan. He loved the blessing basket idea, too. That same month, I sent out an email to the world through Mountain Forum (www.mtnforum.org), asking if there were weavers out there who had a need and desire for this type of work. Overnight I heard from twelve countries, and within two weeks, we were up to twenty-five countries from around the world, receiving eighty individual inquiries about it.

Now the love and support that people showed me in my time of need is being spread worldwide as The Blessing Basket Project® provides sustainable employment and prosperity wages to more than three thousand weavers throughout six countries around the world. The "prosperity wages" we pay refers to the amount of money the weavers get for weaving our baskets. We pay more for these baskets than any organization in the world. We generate thousands of dollars from the sale of these baskets and return the money to local communities through endeavors such as new schools and clean-water projects. The whole mission of the BBP is to reduce world poverty by providing sustainable jobs that pay prosperity wages, *and we're doing it! We wait until we have a good sum (thousands of dollars) to take back to the community, and it's all direct from the sale of baskets. In Ghana, we built a school for little girls with $10,000 we had raised. In Uganda, we have over $5,000 ready to give back, and we're identifying a clean-water project for the community. For Bangladesh, we have $6,000 and are researching the most beneficial project to invest in there. We sold 18,000 baskets in 2007, up from 2,000 baskets in 2004. Our work has become so groundbreaking in the area of poverty reduction that an entire curriculum has been developed around it at Washington University in St. Louis.*

Theresa's childhood experience is not unlike that of many in our world today who have suffered from abuse, neglect, poverty, and despair. But Theresa stands out in that, after she experienced a falling apart in her adult life, she made a bold, powerful choice to use everything that was hers—all the pain, hardship, strength, and determination—to make a real difference in the world, and to reduce the suffering of thousands. Her story reveals that she has "fallen together" after crisis in a way that allows her to be more of who she is—more empowered, more determined, more focused, and more giving. After everything fell apart, Theresa found a new, stronger way to fall together again, a way that represents more powerfully who she is and what she's doing on this planet at this time.

What differentiates someone who is crushed by their life experiences from one who is motivated by them to change the world? The difference is a matter of faith and a matter of choice. Faith is required to believe that all will work out in the end, despite what's appearing in the moment. To believe you will arrive in the light at the end of the tunnel, you have to keep going, keep believing in yourself, keep putting one foot in front of the other, and act—despite your despair—with love, generosity, and empathy. Choice comes into play as you elect to believe *and act on your belief* that somehow you can and do make a difference in this life, that your being here matters. Those who emerge from their falling-apart experiences to make a difference in the lives of others have chosen to trust they are vitally important at this time and place. They are able to move forward with this knowledge in their heart, every moment, every day.

Theresa was very fortunate to have felt love from her mother and grandmother, and to see evidence every day of their amazing courage, strength, and resilience. But luck is not what made Theresa who she is. Who she is emerged from her choices and her decisions to act. Theresa embraced a commitment to let go of her struggles, to stop making excuses, and to be there powerfully for her children and others. She ultimately decided to *be* the change she wanted to see in the world, as Gandhi has so powerfully asked of all of us.

Theresa also displayed the capacity to listen to hard questions, such as her friend's probing "So, what's stopping you?" referring to Theresa's dream to help the world. Those who successfully rise above extreme challenge are those courageous enough to hear what needs to be heard. They listen to positive, expansive guidance from others, get help when necessary, and continue to act from the heart and the gut, accepting that they can and will indeed be powerful, effective vehicles of beneficial change in the world.

Finally, those who successfully overcome a fallen-apart life believe that their past has been useful. Rather than struggle against what they've been given in life, they choose to utilize it all, wasting nothing. They see opportunities when others see only suffering, even in the face of adversity.

Theresa says of her life now: *I believe everyone's life has a meaning and purpose, but I think it's up to each individual to get connected enough to know what they're here to do. For me, this is it, to help women all over the world, and to reduce world poverty in a meaningful way. I believe that this is my purpose. Why did I have to go through divorce, or experience an abusive childhood and the other traumas I faced? I can see now that all of those things cumulatively made me who I am today, made me a survivor, and very compassionate to other hurting people. I couldn't do the work I do today, working with the impoverished, with such feeling if I didn't have the childhood and life I did. It requires a great deal of personal sacrifice to do this work, but my whole life has led up to the purpose of doing what I do today. The Blessing Basket Project® provides me with a fraction of the salary I used to make, and I've downsized my lifestyle to fit the small income. But it is well worth it. If my work weren't to serve the impoverished, it would be another form of service to people I've never met.*

There are women in Uganda who call my husband and me the "sovereigns." They feel we've changed their lives, and they are very humble and grateful. I've been told that they won't even stand up to receive their payment because they are so humbled. I've now been to four of the countries we work with, and I've been so changed by the experience. The Blessing Basket Project® has become so large that, to streamline production and have the best, most positive impact, I must visit the countries directly, and I feel blessed to be able to do so. To meet these beautiful women in person, to hand them their payments and encourage them to stand up to take the money that they've earned—it's such an empowering and soulful experience. In Africa, there are even babies named after me. And the Blessing Basket® has been written into the history of several of the villages. It's my greatest joy and honor to travel there and meet the weavers in person.

I feel so very blessed each and every day. I have a wonderful husband, my beautiful children, and I'm doing work that fills my life with meaning. Today, the original contents of my blessing basket are still there in my living room—the piece of the old tire from my car, my son's old shoe, cards, letters, they're all still there—and I add to my basket regularly still, so thankful for all the blessings of my life. As I look back on my life, I wouldn't change a second of it.

THERESA'S ADVICE

- Don't make excuses. Get out there and change your life. Decide what's important in your life to do, and do it. Rise above what has been.
- Get someone to hold you accountable to make your life visions a reality. Have them ask you, "What's stopping you?" and have them say, "I dare you to make your dream happen."
- Find a powerful role model whom you can look to and learn from. Theresa says, "My mother was my role model—taking care of five adopted kids while her husband was in prison." Find your role model and your inspiration, and follow it.

Stop Making Excuses

We're all very good at making excuses for not taking the actions we dream of. Some, in fact, have become masters at it. "But I've got to pay the bills, don't I?" I hear from so many people who deny their dreams of a passionate, purposeful life. Or "Isn't it impossible to make a difference when the problem is so vast?" folks ask when referring to world problems such as poverty, disease, and war. But where would we be if everyone just let their excuses stand and didn't take action?

Are you aware of the excuses you use to keep you stuck, disempowered, or in the falling-apart mode? Here are some of the insidious excuses I have used or have heard others make for not stepping up to create the life of purpose they long for:

- I'm the breadwinner—I can't risk the financial security I provide.
- I'm a woman—I can only do so much when it comes to this issue.
- I don't have the know-how or experience to make a difference.

- People will say I've lost my mind to take this on.
- It will simply take too long to do what's required—I'll be 60 years old before I'm able to do this.
- I'm already working too hard; I can't take on another thing.
- Focusing on this new direction, even though I want to, seems selfish—I feel like I should be attending to others right now.
- I simply don't have what it takes.
- My husband (friends, family, etc.) won't support me on this.
- How will I find the time or money?
- I've invested so much in where I am now, even though I hate it—I can't shift directions now.
- I really have no idea where to begin.

These are just a few of the many excuses we make to stay where we are, stuck in our meaninglessness. Excuses are a way of connecting with your smallness, your fears, and your lack of trust in yourself. As Theresa says, it's up to each individual to get connected enough to know what they are here to do. I believe that each of us has a strong inkling, from the very beginning, about our reason for being here, but many squelch this inkling as soon as it prompts them to take bold, courageous action.

Do you know what you're here to do? It's time to get hip to your trip, identify the excuses you're making today for not doing what you long to, and let them go.

Get Someone to Hold You Accountable

Theresa found in her friend someone who loved her enough to call her up short. "So, what's stopping you?" her friend asked when Theresa told her she longed to help the world. This sort of friend is someone who knows what you're capable of, hears and connects with your deepest longings, and trusts you have what it takes to achieve what you yearn for. How blessed we'd be if we all had friends like this! But many of us don't.

If you don't, make no excuses about it. Find a new friend, or discover a coach or mentor, someone who can hold you up to the image of your future self and ask you to embrace it. This individual must view life expansively, believe in your empowerment, and trust without doubt that you can and will be all you wish to be in life.

People who invest and believe in you also encourage you to be accountable for your actions, for your life. They bring out your courage, fortitude, and determination to get through anything and rise above. Find someone who believes in you without limit, and have them say, "I dare you!" to make your dreams come true.

Find a Powerful Role Model

Theresa had in her mother and grandmother role models of loving women who were strong, determined, positive, and proactive. Many women aren't so lucky—their mothers or other women in their lives didn't serve as powerfully positive forces. If that was your situation, don't let it remain an excuse for you not stepping forward. Powerful role models are everywhere; you just have to find one that resonates for you.

I recall being asked many years ago who my role models were, and I hadn't a clue. I couldn't think of one individual, past or present, I wished to emulate or learn from. This lack said much more about me than I realized. I was disconnected from the world, cut off, angry, resentful, and arrogant, as if I had nothing to learn from anyone. It also revealed that I was disconnected from myself—I remained unaware of my deep longings to help and be helped. I was struggling to survive in a world that was false to me, and I felt that no one could understand or come to my aid. But I was wrong.

Recently, I began to read about women who've made a difference in the world and fell upon the teachings and writings of Mother Teresa. I was captivated, moved, and stunned by the enormous impact of this one small woman. Her compassion and love for those who suffer and for the world's outcasts and the poor still rock me to my core. I was touched, too, that she remained full of human frailty, as we all are, and secretly suffered from doubts about her faith and about the existence of God. She is someone I greatly admire because her words and thoughts are overflowing with love, forgiveness, and acceptance—aspects of the human experience that I deeply long to expand in myself. It has been said that what you admire in others exists in you; otherwise, you wouldn't recognize it. I believe this is true. Find someone to admire and emulate, and you will find yourself again.

MOVING FORWARD TO BREAKTHROUGH

✳ STEP BACK

- Think about your past, your childhood and early teens. Did that time involve deep struggle? What was the nature of that struggle (was it with the world, money, people, illness, circumstance)? How did you and your family manage?
- How is struggle part of your life today?

- How is it part of your concept of who you are?
- Are you willing to let the past be the past with regard to struggle?
- Are you ready, beginning today, to say and feel, "I know what is important in my life and work, and honor that with ease; I have released my connection to struggle"? Say this affirmation out loud every morning for a month. Write in your journal about your experiences of giving up the struggle and embracing ease, once and for all.

✳ LET GO of making excuses.

In your journal, capture all your thoughts. *No censoring, please—write everything that comes to mind.*

- What excuses do you use most to remain stuck?
- Your biggest excuse in life is _____.
- From whom did you learn these excuses? Who from your past was good at using the same excuses? How did these excuses hold him/her back?
- How are your excuses holding you back?
- If you knew that these excuses were there simply to mask your fears about moving forward, how willing would you be to let them go?
- What one step can you take this week to stop making excuses and start doing . . . moving forward in the face of your fears?

✳ SAY YES! to creating your new life as you want it.

Recommended Steps

1. Find inspiring role models.

- Seek out and research two people, one in your community and one elsewhere, whom you admire.
- Write down all the traits, behaviors, thinking, and characteristics that draw you to this individual. What makes this person special in your mind?
- Now explore these characteristics *in you*: How and when have you displayed these qualities? How do you wish to bring them forward? What do you dream to be and do, using these qualities?

- Ask to interview the inspiring individual in your community. Ask them to explain how they moved forward, step by step, toward their life visions. What did they have access to (in themselves and otherwise) that helped? Bring to light all the qualities they possess that *you also share*. Realize you're not so different from that person.

2. Find someone to hold you accountable.

- Find a friend, a coach, or a mentor who has an expansive, empowered view of you and of life itself, someone who can help you be accountable for taking action that moves you forward toward a life of greater purpose and joy.
- Meet with your friend/coach regularly (weekly or monthly) to help you explore your visions, set goals, share your progress, and move you through your obstacles.
- Ask your coach to dare you to make your dream a reality. Give him/her permission to ask as many times as necessary, "What's stopping you?" to keep you true to your visions.

Remember

Choosing to make full use of everything life has given you, rather than breaking yourself against it, is the difference between living fully and meaningfully, and staying stuck in suffering. It's a choice. Only you can make it.

Theresa reminds us

"Your life makes you who you are. Either you'll fall victim for the rest of your life, or you're going to rise above it and use what's happened to make your life a better place. I would not change one second of what I've been through."

✳ **BREAKTHROUGH** "I know what is important to me, and I honor it."

14

Balancing Life and Work

Being responsible for my life, my children, my choices sustains me even in the darkest hours.

LESLIE MORGAN STEINER
Mommy Wars

* **STEP BACK TO EXPLORE** Overfunctioning and perfectionism to control your world.

* **LET GO** of your fears about not being in control.

* **SAY YES!** to being helped by others and your higher self.

* **BREAKTHROUGH**
"I balance my life and work with joy."

Because balancing life and work is one of the most prevalent crises for working women today, this chapter offers two compelling stories about real-life professionals who have achieved balance and harmony and inspire others to do the same.

* **Karen:** *When I think about childhood, I realize now that I was deeply formed by my culture and upbringing. My mom was a traditional wife and mother—a corporate executive's wife—and Dad was a high-powered successful executive. I grew up in suburbia, and somewhere I got the message that I needed to go it on my own, be independent, tough it out, go do it. I felt I needed to be successful monetarily or something was wrong with me. Either you married success, or you did it yourself—that's what made you worthwhile. Looking back now, I see that it was huge ingrained fear—I felt as if I were going to die if I didn't have money.*

From early on, I had artistic ability and was interested in fine arts and design. So I went to art school, then moved to Boston and got a neat job in the interior design field. I worked there for five years and really enjoyed it. Then I got laid off. I really didn't know what to do from there. I was in my early 20s and somehow—I don't know where it came from—I realized I was attracted to the food business. I got the idea that I wanted to start a wholesale baking company, selling individual desserts to hotels and restaurants.

From nothing, I started this baking company. My parents gave me a bit of seed money, and over the years, I built up my business and was successful. Eventually I had an opportunity to sell the business and sold it to a big company and made some great money. After that, I poked around trying to land on something that appealed to me. I really didn't know

* Karen (not her real name) is a 50-year-old consultant at a leading natural and organic foods supermarket.

what I wanted to do. I did some consulting for food businesses, then I got off on a tangent that I wanted to open up a bakery-café. My partner backed out at the last minute. After that, I was really at a loss about my next move.

Karen's culturally given concepts about success were wrapped up in the notion that, to be worthwhile, you must make or marry money. That urgent need, sensed but unstated, was fueled by her underlying fear that if she didn't gain access to wealth, she'd be a failure. Many women experience this driving fear. The prevalent definition of "success equals money" often gives birth to the negative belief that "I am nothing without money."

Karen continues: *My sister worked at a leading natural foods supermarket at the time, and she told me about a job as a team leader in one of the stores and suggested I go for it. I said, "Are you nuts? I don't want to work in a supermarket!" I'd had my own successful business, had been a free agent. She, my husband, and my mother all teamed up and told me, "We think you should really interview for this job, it might be very good for you. Do it for a year and see." So I gave it a try.*

Turns out I was like a duck to water at this job. I was able to use my artistic eye and merchandising skills to make this department and others look striking and beautiful. The job evolved and expanded, and I was really successful. I was in the role for five years. As the years went on, I climbed from team leader to head merchandiser, flying all over the country. I was recognized for my skills, so I'd open other stores—I'd go to San Francisco, Chicago, then New York, all over. I probably opened up fifteen stores and did this work for nine years.

Then, three years ago, the company changed and began to expand exponentially. My daughter was 5 at that point and very attached to me—still is to this day, and I to her. But I'd find a way to do it, to leave and go do my work, travel, whatever was required. I'd hold my breath each time and force myself to walk out the door. But once I was gone I was okay. The longest period I could ever bear being away was five days straight. My husband and I would work out getting the family together after that if my travels took me away for longer. We figured out how to work it, but it always ripped my heart out, and my little daughter suffered, too.

At that point, I also saw the landscape of the company changing. My work was getting a lot more demanding, and they were talking about opening stores throughout Europe. I'd have to take on international travel, and more and more demands that would take me away from my family.

At the same time as this, my husband, who had been doing much of the caregiving of our daughter and had gone back to law school, began working full-time. I knew in my soul that we wanted the type of family situation that would involve my husband and I caring for our daughter, and avoid having a nanny if we could. But I also wanted to support my husband. This may sound sexist, but the truth is, the way we're both wired, I believed deep down that I needed to step back a bit so he could have his day. He's been a lot more insecure about himself and his success level than I have. I began to wonder to myself, "Maybe it's time to step back a little bit, to be less in the spotlight, and let him have his time."

Karen had begun to achieve everything she ever dreamed of. Her job was exciting, creative, and full of high-level responsibility, which would have made her parents proud. But the very job that she loved and that gave her great self-esteem also stole her away from her daughter, and each time it did, it was excruciating. Karen also began to feel as if her all-consuming success might be holding her husband back from succeeding.

Karen continues: *My husband's practice began to pick up a bit, with more commitments on his time, leaving him less flexible to care for our daughter. So here we are, three years ago. I'm working incredibly demanding hours in my big job, with stress, travel, heart-wrenching departures from my daughter, the works. I was loving my success but finding it very hard to balance the other parts of my life. One day three events were happening for my daughter— a dance recital, a school event, and a sports event—and I just couldn't get any of the day right. After the third event, I said, "This is insane!" I couldn't figure out which end was up.*

Finally, I couldn't take it. I had a mini nervous breakdown. I could feel it building for days, but I wasn't sure what was going on inside me. One day, I was driving to an offsite meeting, and all of a sudden, I began to cry uncontrollably. I had no idea what was going on with me, but I simply couldn't stop crying. I had to call my boss and say, "I'm so sorry, but I can't do this. I can't come to this meeting." I was so stressed, and again that day it had been hard to leave my daughter, but nothing in particular happened that day to break me down. I was just a complete mess. I couldn't handle it.

I then decided to take a six-week leave of absence to get my head together. I truly didn't know which end was up. It was a complete shock. I'm a lot more in touch with myself and my emotions now, but back then I was clueless. I was like a superwoman. My husband said I was workaholic—my idea of quality time with my daughter was having her sit beside me while I worked on my laptop. I worked every waking second. A friend once said, "What is it with you? Why do you have to do everything, be great at everything?" I was great at everything except for taking care of myself, and prioritizing in my life what really mattered most—my daughter and my family, along with my health and well-being, all of which I desperately needed to address.

Karen's mini nervous breakdown blindsided her. This type of breakdown is all too common for women who are highly driven, compelled to be successful, and forced by their own beliefs to do everything perfectly. Not listening to her husband or friends, Karen persisted in attempting to balance the impossible—extreme work demands along with her needs to be intimately connected with her family. Her story reminds us of an important truth—when we try over and over to do the impossible, not getting that it's not working, life has a way of intervening. In Karen's case, it brought her to breakdown.

So I got help, and began to see a therapist. It was clear that it was time to step off this treadmill. I said to my boss, "I can't come back to my job. We need to find something else to do," which we did. I became the regional buyer—moved sideways, with similar pay, and compensation and status, but an office job. I could stay local, not travel. All was well for a bit, but then they started asking again for a little travel, to help them open the New Jersey store, the New York store. Six months into this job, I had to go open a store in another state and be there a whole week. I was miserable. One day—the last straw—I got in the car to come home and went the wrong way on the highway. I burst into tears and screamed on the phone to a friend, "I don't want to do this! I feel like I'm going to have another nervous breakdown." By August I said to myself, "I'm done." I gave my notice—without anything in the wings. They offered me some suggestions, but I didn't want any of their options.

Six months before that, I had started to receive energy healing work, and it was very powerful. I was searching for something other than therapy and was always attracted to spirituality but never surrendered to it. I was always too busy. The energy healing work I've experienced has completely changed my life. And I started to see a coach as well. But I didn't want a coach to teach me to be the president of the company. I wanted a life coach who could help me to connect with my spirituality and gain balance and perspective, too. Our coaching sessions did that, and were wonderful.

Through all this inner work, I turned myself inside and out, got very real with myself. I looked at what I had originally feared most (being a "nothing" if I wasn't tremendously successful) and discovered what mattered most to me. I finally was able to let go of the need to be the master of everything. Finally I took action that supported what's important to me—time with my daughter, helping support my husband be all he could be. In doing so, something amazing happened. I ended up launching this incredible project for the company. This project is so from the heart. It's huge, and it has the capability of changing people's lives. It makes a real difference in the world. I see now that inside me there's passion and caring for the world. But before, it was completely buried. When I got in touch with the knowledge that this project is going to change people's lives, that's when it all came together.

When you finally decide to be real with yourself, face down your fears, and do the work required to act on what you care about most, miraculous shifts occur. Gifts come to you in the form of ease, purpose, balance, and joy. By stepping up for her needs as a mother, wife, and individual, Karen finally walked off the treadmill of her extreme job. She created the necessary space to receive the soulful gift of developing a world-changing project. Her commitment to herself finally made possible what she had longed for most—a purposeful, exciting career that allows her to be all she wants to be, in a way that works for her.

Karen's life now: *I'm living very differently now. I have a home office and work from home regularly. I'm not attached at the hip to my laptop anymore, and I'm dedicated to spending quality time with my husband and daughter. I'm exercising, eating well, I've lost twenty pounds, and I'm really taking care of myself. I'm with my family as I need and want to be. And my husband is very successful and happy, too. It's a completely different life. I'm off the treadmill now. And I'm doing work that brings fulfillment and purpose to my life.*

I don't get that sinking feeling of emptiness anymore. I feel I'm here for a purpose, and that purpose is much bigger than myself and my family. I've looked at these fears now about needing to be the best, be wealthy, and handle everything perfectly. I've exposed them and overcome them. I don't make the money I used to, but my hope is that I will someday, but do it with less stress, so I can continue to have a family life that is balanced, calm, and happy. I don't feel scared about it anymore. I trust that I'm not alone in this, that my husband is in this with me. We have savings, we've put away money for the future. I know my husband couldn't be the equal I longed for unless I stepped back to allow space for that. I'm so excited about where I am now. I'm very grateful for what I have in my life. It all fits together beautifully.

KAREN'S ADVICE

- Stop overfunctioning, and align yourself with your priorities.
- Find out what you fear most and address it.
- Get help from others and your spiritual self to take back your life.

Stop Overfunctioning

Karen discovered the ultimate belief that drove her actions—she would be a "nothing" if she were not wealthy. This belief pushed her to run herself ragged. Such fear-based beliefs drive women to become overfunctioners. They take on a slew of responsibilities, chores, and projects that do not match what truly matters to them at their core. They feel they "have" to do all this to be validated, accepted, or loved. In the process they lose themselves.

Women have been chronically overfunctioning for years, ever since they emerged on the work scene and were charged with the overwhelming tasks of balancing work and family responsibilities. Overfunctioning means taking on more than is required or necessary, more than is possible. I should know—I'm a recovering overfunctioner.

What drives women to overfunction? Believing that if you don't overfunction, something bad will occur: I'll miss out on a critical development if I'm not always there; someone else (my husband, for instance) will do it wrong; my children's welfare will be jeopardized; I'll be ridiculed if I don't do everything; I'll be seen as "less than" others; or, finally, if I can't be the best at both worlds, I'm an abject failure.

Women typically have overly full plates. Research shows that women still take on the lion's share of domestic responsibilities, even if they work, and even when they are the primary breadwinners. This overload is extremely difficult to manage. As Leslie Morgan Steiner, editor of the important and compelling book *Mommy Wars*,[1] explained to me, she found balancing work and family torturous at times. She admitted candidly that she wished she hadn't had to face the obstacles she did—namely, being forced to give up her exciting and fulfilling sixty-plus-hour-a-week job running the *Washington Post* and reducing her hours and salary by 50 percent, in order to carve out the precious family time that was critical to her.

So what can we do about our overly full plates and our tendency to overfunction? We have the power to change this dynamic. It boils down to prioritizing with conviction what matters most to you, then shifting your focus away from what matters less. Shed the need to do it all perfectly. Embrace help from all those who will give it. And learn to trust that you are not meant to handle *everything* yourself. Take action today to ask and empower others—your spouse, children, colleagues, subordinates, etc.—to take on more responsibility, wherever possible and appropriate. An essential corollary to this is to free yourself from guilt about getting help, to remember that getting help is a way of saying yes! to yourself.

If you find this shift in attitude and behavior challenging, you need to examine why you believe you're the only one who can do all that you're doing. Get support from someone outside yourself, and your higher self, to see what's holding you hostage, keeping you chained to your need to do it all, and perfectly. This type of honest self-exploration leads to discovering past traumas and subconscious beliefs that no longer serve you. Perhaps your childhood was insecure, and your parents weren't reliable or there for you, leaving you feeling frightened and alone. Maybe your parents and teachers demanded perfection, withholding acceptance or love unless you showed them evidence of your perfection. Or perhaps your self-esteem was so beaten down that being in control or perfect was the only way you knew how to survive. Explore today what keeps you in overfunctioning mode. What actions can you take to step off the treadmill? What can you do to slow down the pace so that you are living in harmony with what matters most to you?

Address What You Fear Most

While fear sometimes motivates us to change, it can also keep us stuck. Karen's fear of parental rejection and the belief that wealth equals worthiness kept her in exhausting overdrive. My fears that bad things would happen if I weren't controlling everything at home kept me rageful and worn out. We all have fears. They are a necessary and helpful component of human existence. But the more locked away your fears are from your conscious thought, they more they drive you to behave in unsatisfying, self-destructive, and limiting ways—without your awareness or consent. If you are finding it impossible to balance life and work, look at your deepest fears. How are they driving you, limiting you, and wearing you out?

What are you most afraid of? Following are areas and questions that elicit fear, anxiety, or pain for many individuals I've worked with.

From the Past:

- Relationships that broke your heart
- "Failure" to succeed or perform
- Being criticized, rejected, or ridiculed
- Being told you were "not enough"
- Being negatively compared with others
- Being abused and mistreated
- Being envied or despised for your successes
- Bringing about harm or suffering to others
- Being alone and frightened

In the Present:

- Dealing with current responsibilities—can I do it?
- Keeping your family safe and secure in today's world
- Feeling like you don't matter
- Dealing with financial worries
- Coping with disease and illnesses
- Feeling numb, depressed, and cut off
- Keeping your flaws a secret
- Feeling or acting out of control
- Fearing you are falling apart

In the Future:

- Will I find and keep love? Am I lovable?
- Will I handle my challenges without blowing it?
- Do I have what it takes?
- Can I take care of myself and my family?
- Will my children be secure and successful?
- Will I be safe and secure?
- Will I live a long and healthy life?
- Will I be destitute and homeless?
- Will I be alone?
- Will I survive this?
- Will the world survive this?

What do you fear most? Death, rejection, success, pain, exposure, sadness, separation? Bring this fear into your awareness. Talk to it. Get to know it. Live with it. Confront what frightens you the most, and embrace it as a friend. Allow it to exist in the light of day. Only then will you be able to walk away from it, with power and surety, if fragments and images of it reappear in your life.

Get Help from Others and Your Higher Self

Coaching and energy healing helped Karen get in touch with her spiritual side in a life-changing way. She found help from her coach and healer, as well as from her spiritual voice and practices. These aids grounded her in a new reality of calm, balance, and acceptance. Many women find strength and solace by getting in closer touch with their spiritual being.

There are many helpful ways to find your spiritual self. Spiritual beliefs and practices that connect you more fully to yourself, enhance your self-respect and compassion for others, help you feel your own power and divinity, and appreciate the vastness of human experience are highly beneficial.

But many of us were taught religious beliefs that hold us back and simply don't ring true. I know I was. And I threw the baby out with the bathwater. If this statement strikes a chord, I encourage you to seek out new spiritual beliefs and practices that feel right to you. Keep the baby! Find a way to connect to your spiritual side, and to something more expansive than your individual self. Doing so brings great perspective and peace of mind.

When I began to search for spiritual concepts that would bolster rather than frustrate me, I found a fascinating book, *Conversations with God*, by Neale Donald Walsch.[2] I devoured it in one night. For the first time in my life, I felt like I was home. I finally read in print spiritual ideas that feel right, beautiful, loving, and true. I was overjoyed. Since then, I have continued to build spiritual beliefs that support and nourish me. Connecting to your spiritual side, hearing your inner voice, and living from the knowledge you receive will get you closer to your values and priorities, soothe you, and set you in a positive direction with courage and power.

Getting help from other people in your life is also essential. If managing everything on your plate is impossible, reach out and ask for help. I love a concept I learned in my therapy training: "Never do for others what they can do for themselves." When we overdo for others, we rob them—our children, spouses, or colleagues, friends, and employees—of precious opportunities to directly experience their own competence and power. To get new balance in your life and work, ask for (insist on) help now. Who might be able to step up, handle more, take something off your plate, today? Who can lighten your load? Who in your life will step up to their own power and potential by handling what rightfully belongs to them? By encouraging their self-reliance, you'll be doing them an enormous service—and creating needed space in your life as well.

*   *   *

Sandy's story below offers another wonderful example of overcoming limitations, and finding a new, balanced approach to meaningful living and working. Sandy took on her fears, let go of perfectionism, and came out the other side reinvented. Her story inspires other leaders and professionals to do the same.

* **Sandy:** *My deepest crisis occurred thirteen years ago. I was married, in what I had convinced myself was a perfectly good relationship, with a perfectly good family life, and a perfectly forever situation. Then it happened—my marriage ended. My children were 1 and 3 years old at the time. I was working part-time in human resources and working non-stop to make everything "perfect."*

I realize now that my relationship with my husband had disintegrated over time, and frankly, I disintegrated along with it. My need to do everything perfectly got in the way of my seeing reality. Things got so bad for me that at one point I had to shoot myself in the leg regularly with medication for my intense headaches. I was so unhealthy, thin. You wouldn't know that to look at me now . . . I'm 43, strong, healthy, and in good condition. But it was very different then. Balancing with perfection the whole of my life—my work, children, my falling-apart relationship, my financial worries, my health—it just wasn't doable any longer.

My husband left the house, and we separated for a year. After seven months of counseling, and a tremendous amount of self-exploration and self-discovery, I learned that he was fine with the way it was, fine with our lifestyle, our relationship, but I wasn't fine with any of it. We've divorced and he's since remarried, and we have an amicable relationship now.

I remember after my husband left me, I was sitting in the blue chair in our old house. On the floor was a brown file box filled with all our financial documents. That box sat there on the floor with the top on for the longest time, until one day I finally drew up the courage to open it. I looked at all the papers inside and promptly threw up. It just was all too much. I knew then that my life couldn't work this way a moment longer. Balancing my family's

* Sandy Sullivan is a 43-year-old co–program manager for diversity in a Fortune 100 company.

needs with work and financial demands just wasn't going to be possible the way I'd done it before.

Something in me knew that life wasn't supposed to be just about surviving. "Ease" did not describe my typical way of being, but I trusted that ease could be in my future—and I began searching for ways to let ease in. I embarked on a transformational period, turning myself inside out to discover myself. I studied, explored, questioned; went to talks and seminars; read books; and jumped into experiencing myself fully.

I also took on those things that scared me to death. For instance, I called my father and said, "I love you and I hate you." I even did a tandem sky dive—to directly confront my relationship with fear. I believe it's not enough to become aware of what you fear, you have to get into the cage with it. Sweat, cry, get right up on top of it. And that's what I did.

After undergoing a long period of many experiential encounters, I can say, thirteen years later, that I finally know what acceptance and forgiveness mean. I confronted myself, opened myself up and closed it down, over and over again. During this time, and now, my spiritual practices have helped me tremendously—helped me see and accept who I am, and let others be who they are, and to go with the flow.

Professionally, I consulted part-time in HR after my divorce until 1996 to pay the bills. But then I joined a colleague of mine at a great company in an extraordinary job-share position in organizational training and development. We've job-shared for twelve years and currently serve as joint program manager for diversity for the company. We are very unified in this role and help each other tremendously, both personally and professionally. My whole purpose in work today is to unleash women from what I call "the significance of corporate America." My belief is that your whole, integrated life is what is significant, and that you mustn't sacrifice yourself to your corporate existence.

I co-deliver leadership training courses all over the world now. In these courses, we explore the broken-down process that many leaders go through today, of trying to balance "What I want" with "What I should do for the company." Instead, we encourage asking, "What do I want?" and "What does the company want?' paired with the critical exploration of how to create the "AND" in that equation—the common ground between them.

My work now is an outgrowth of all I went through. I'm blessed to be working as I do, in a job-share situation with a friend I deeply care about. We're very fortunate that the company supports this. This arrangement allows us to split our travel and work demands so that we both can manage our personal responsibilities, yet deliver on-the-job requirements in the way we feel comfortable.

I don't think I would have been successful in this job-share position before my crisis, but now I have a different life view. I am much more able to go with the flow; I'm less perfectionistic. I'm far more accepting of who I am and the bumps in life, and of change. Some would even call me "loosey goosey." Being of service matters to me a great deal, and I'm blessed to have a job that fulfills that need. I'm able to balance my life and work well now, in great part because I have a deep and supportive relationship with my job-share partner. Working in this collaborative, balanced way means the world to me.

Sandy's story offers similar guidance as Karen's for finding true balance in life and work.

SANDY'S ADVICE

- Get clear about what matters to you, and live from that knowledge.
- Take on your fears—get in the cage with them to resolve them.
- Get help from others and your spiritual self to reclaim your life.

MOVING FORWARD TO BREAKTHROUGH

✳ STEP BACK

In your journal, capture all your thoughts. *No censoring, please—write everything that comes to mind.*

- What is your deepest fear about not being perfect at everything you do?
- What is your deepest fear about giving up some control?
- What is your deepest fear about not being able to handle everything you're handling?
- What would a truly *balanced* life look and feel like, for you?

✳ **LET GO** of your fears about not being in control.

How can you bring your fears forward and "get in the cage" with them today? Consider some suggestions:

- Have a conversation with the one person from your past you most want approval from, and tell them you are giving up your need for their approval. (If possible, have this conversation in person face-to-face. If conversing is not possible, imagine the conversation in your mind, vividly.)
- Do something that you'd love to do but are deeply afraid to (like Sandy's sky dive)—sing in front of someone, do some public speaking, display your artwork, do a high dive, or take a skiing lesson.
- Come up with three things that your spouse, children, family members, friends, or coworkers can do to support you and lighten your load. Tell them you need their help.
- Research and explore what it would mean for you to revise your work life or cut back at work to accommodate what you want in your personal life. What would be required to move forward on that front?
- Identify the one person in life who wants you to *stop* being in complete control of everything. Ask them what they truly want from you. Does what they want sound good to you? If so, move toward it.

Take action to honor yourself by addressing your deepest fear in regard to balancing life and work today.

✳ **SAY YES!** to being helped by others and your higher self.

Recommended Steps

1. Sit quietly, breathe deeply, and think about what matters most to you. Ask yourself:

   - What are my life priorities? Who and what really matter to me in my life?
   - What do I long to be really good at, and what do I want focus on, going forward?

- What can I live with giving up, or being *okay* at?
- What specifically is causing me to feel like I can't balance life and work?
- What shifts can I make to address this? (For instance, who isn't pulling their weight in my life? What help can I receive?)

2. Based on your insights from the above questions, complete this exercise:

- My long-term priorities are: _____

  _____

- My short-term priorities are: _____

  _____

- What these priorities have in common (the "AND"): _____

  _____

- How are they different, and what can I do about the gap? _____

  _____

3. Now consider your spiritual beliefs and practices.

- What are my spiritual beliefs? Make a full list.
- How do they help me, in life and work? How might my existing beliefs be holding me back?
- Which of my spiritual beliefs need to be reexamined, modified, or released?
- What can I do this month to:

  - Embrace and develop spiritual beliefs that resonate with me more *personally* and *directly*?
  - Shed those that don't?
  - Apply my spiritual beliefs practically, in my daily life?

4. Take one step this week to:

- Get clear about what matters most to you
- Address your fears
- Ask someone for help in lightening your load

Remember

Despite challenges that we women face to balance life and work, there's never been a better time to be here, to step up to what matters most, and to act from that self-knowledge.

Karen reminds us

"That decision to step away was truly life-changing for me. I've made peace with it because it fits me and what I need. The change in my life addresses my personal needs but also reflects something much bigger. I had to have this crisis in order to be ready to take on this life-changing project. Now I don't feel scared about anything anymore. I trust that I'm not alone in this, and I also trust that we have everything we need."

✳ **BREAKTHROUGH** "I balance my life and work with joy."

15

Doing Work and Play You Love

It is very dangerous to go into eternity with
possibilities which one has oneself prevented
from becoming realities. A possibility is
a hint from God. One must follow it.

SØREN KIERKEGAARD

EMPOWERMENT WITH HIGHER SELF

Laura: *From as early as I can remember, I knew I wanted to perform. So as soon as I could, I went to New York City to study acting, dance, and theater. I went to New York on a dance scholarship and was seriously intending to pursue theater and acting full-time. But truthfully, after a few years I became tired of just scraping by with very little money. I'd always loved writing, too, so I decided to go back to school and get a degree in writing and philosophy at NYU, and see where that would take me. When I graduated, somehow a switch got thrown in my head. A huge shift occurred inside me. Suddenly I said to myself, "You have got to stop being a child and go to work full-time. Stop playing around and get serious." A lot of this was my parents' influence, I think. While they've been supportive of my talents and abilities, they've always wanted me to be pragmatic about career reality. Trying to be helpful, they communicated the idea that acting is a really difficult business. And that one has to be realistic. It's not that they ever said I wasn't good enough, but they impressed upon me that I had to be realistic and take care of myself.*

So I listened. In the 1990s, I began pursuing the corporate route full-time, in the publishing and book club fields, but I still couldn't completely give up acting. I was doing off-Broadway plays for no money, rehearsing and doing shows in the evenings and working full-time during the day. I'd do one or two productions a year, nothing huge. I was also in a band, and we performed periodically, and made an album in the early '90s. I wrote short stories and monologues, too.

But as the years wore on, more and more time was siphoned away from creative work to my corporate existence. The thing about it was that when I got to work, it wasn't terrible. I wasn't totally miserable. I became engaged with my projects, the people were nice, it was fine. By three in the afternoon I'd be completely drained and exhausted and want

✳ Laura (not her real name), 40, a former book club editor and web marketing manager, is currently an actress, singer, and screenwriter.

191

to go to bed, but by seven I was happy to get out of work and I'd have all this energy again. The corporate environment was very structured, and the work was not challenging. It was mostly about showing up. Frankly, if I had been more miserable, I think I would have spent fewer years treading water, stuck in this empty life. But I just stayed. Sure, I had the typical stomachache every Sunday night. I also had the feeling of real loss of personal freedom, and knowing that this life wasn't really what I wanted. And I kept wondering to myself why I just couldn't do what I wanted to, but I didn't take any action to make a real change.

Laura's story resembles thousands I've heard. She emerged from childhood knowing exactly what she wanted to do. She developed her skills and gave it a good go. But when the going got tough, as it will, doubt and discouragement kicked in, as did the voices of authority in her life. They hinted at the rightness of giving up her dream because it was potentially too hard a life, too much of a stretch to believe it would work out well.

Laura gets new guidance and follows a dream: *Then something amazing occurred. I was working full-time until 1997, when I got a call out of the blue from a theater producer I'd worked with ten years earlier in California. He ran a theater where I met my husband. He called and said, "I know you're not doing theater professionally now, but I'd love you to come out this summer. I've got this great play you should do. I want you to choreograph the kids' musical . . . you'll love it." His phone call had a huge impact on me. I was really rocked by the idea that I could actually go and do this.*

When I got his call, though, I almost dismissed it, thinking, "That's not what you do anymore. You just can't up and quit your job." But a little voice inside, like an angel's voice, or a form of guidance or higher consciousness, told me, "You really should pay attention to this." For whatever reason, I heeded that voice. I took the leap, quit my job, and went out to L.A. for three months.

I had the most amazing time ever. It was so stimulating, rewarding, a blast, and the whole creative environment was fantastic. It reminded me of how happy I had been working at this theater years earlier. I was a performer and choreographer, and working longer days than ever before. But I felt so much more alive and happy. As the time wound down to return, I really dreaded going back to New York. I thought, "Now I have to stop loving life and go back to the real world." I didn't for a second entertain the idea that maybe I didn't have to go back. So I returned and got back into freelance copywriting at my old place of work, three days a week.

Not surprisingly, I got very depressed. I gained a lot of weight, and over time, my back problems began to worsen. I have scoliosis, which had always been manageable, but during this time it grew more severe and painful. I started going to psychotherapy then for some help, and it helped me see the root of my problems—my therapist was the physical embodiment of my inner voice and she gave it credence. It took me years to follow my inner voice, but I eventually did it. The next summer, the theater wanted me back, and I returned and loved every second of it.

Again, I begrudgingly returned to New York after the summer, still working part-time freelance at the book club company. I pursued other theater work, but I was still mired in the idea that I couldn't give acting 100 percent of my effort. I began to realize that a lot of why I was tied to this empty existence was because of my marriage and the role I was playing in it. I began to realize that my husband and I had drifted apart, and together we had developed a dynamic that was keeping me in an unhappy environment. I wanted to change the contract—emotionally, financially, and in terms of career. In many ways, I was moving away from him and from our original vision of our life together.

We went to couples therapy, tried to talk this out . . . because we loved each other. I felt really guilty and overwhelmed at the idea that I was moving away from my happiness being tied up with him, or in having a house and family together. It's funny, we just kept saying, "Let's try this, or let's try that." We bought a house together, and I tried desperately to get pregnant but couldn't. I stayed in the house eight months, and as much as I loved the house, I didn't want to do it anymore. I was working four days a week as an independent consultant, developing websites for book clubs, and I felt really bored and disconnected. I took a thirty-minute train ride each way, meditating every morning and every night about my life.

I thought I was meditating about getting pregnant, getting clarity and guidance about it, and that it was going to bring me a child. But in actuality the clarity brought me the realization that I couldn't stay in the house, in the marriage, or in this empty life one second longer. That voice was in my head again, saying, "Laura, there's no physical reason that you aren't getting pregnant. The reason you are not pregnant is that this is not the life you're meant to be leading." So I decided I had to leave.

The inner voice that Laura heard gave her surprising and challenging information. Her inability to get pregnant was in fact serving her, pushing her forward to finally leave her unhappy life behind. Your inner voice urges you to overcome all the obstacles you've created for yourself. It asks that you trust that you have an important reason for being here. Your inner voice also honors your life purpose by urging you to take bold action to support it.

Leaving an unhappy life behind: *I took it one step at a time, got a divorce in May 2001. And then 9/11 happened. An acquaintance of mine was an actress who was temping in an office on the 99th floor of the World Trade Center, and she didn't make it out. I personally had a view of the whole event from our office window, and like so many, I had to walk home to Brooklyn that day. It took seven hours. I was covered in dust, traumatized, shaken to the bone. I had a "come to Jesus moment," as they say, during my walk home—I asked myself, "How do you spend your time, your life? Days turn into weeks and years in a split second. I've made this change, gotten a divorce, and I'm recovering. Where do I want to be next year, the year after that?" My guidance voice reemerged and told me I should move to Los Angeles. But I was so resistant. My training was in theater, not television or film. Every time I'd go to L.A. to visit my friends, I'd think, "L.A. is a toilet, a pigsty." In some ways, I didn't want to leave New York because I felt loyal. Especially after 9/11. It felt like we were all at a funeral, and you don't just get up and leave a funeral until it's time to leave. But finally, moving to L.A. made sense to me, for my career and for my life. So I set a goal of doing it within a year, and started saving money.*

In March 2003, I moved. And the oddest thing happened. From the minute I arrived, L.A. felt like home. It's still a toilet, but it's my toilet. I underwent terrifying life changes, but I felt like I had my family in my corner. When I finally took charge and said, "This is what I'm going to do and I need to know that you believe in me and are behind me," my family supported me without hesitation.

I have an amazing fiancé now, Rex, a gifted actor, producer, and entrepreneur. He's so generous, loving, and, maybe most important, spiritually connected. I'm so happy in this relationship. I spent eight months in L.A. not being with anyone, and I am grateful for having that time alone. I found out that I'm good on my own. I realized I could say for the first time ever, "I like what I'm doing, the person I am. I'm complete." And as soon as I started making these big life changes, my body changed, too. It sounds like a Hollywood script, but the minute I left my husband and my unfulfilling life and work, my back got so much better. Being happier made my body happier, too.

Laura's story is a beautiful, classic example of a journey from breakdown to breakthrough. Despairing in a career that didn't fit, missing her creative life, and despondent in a marriage that began as supportive but shifted over time, she had a "breakdown"—which took a serious toll on her physical and emotional health. But through the regular practice of her train-ride meditation, she receives direction. Her inner voice tells her that there's a profoundly meaningful reason she's not getting pregnant, and that reason is that she is to walk away from the life and career she's built, and reclaim the life she desires—of creativity, fulfillment, and well-being.

Finally, the realization of what she needed to do—move to L.A. and pursue acting again—came to her once more through her inner guidance, offered to her as she endured the crisis of 9/11. The cataclysmic life trauma of 9/11 woke Laura up (as it did thousands of others) to claiming a life of passion, power, and purpose. Once she did so, the world supported her every move.

Making it as an actress: *I've thrown myself into the life and pursuit of a working actor. I'm writing all the time, doing plays, and getting casting people to come. I've written a one-woman show and co-written a sketch comedy show that I performed at Second City, and I've co-starred on* Desperate Housewives, *and several other television shows. Just recently, I submitted a screenplay that has been very well received, and there's another one on the way.*

When I moved out here, I had no connections, no agent, no film and TV resume, no reel, and I was in my late 30s. So I just got up every day and did something substantial toward getting my name in front of casting people. I try to meet everyone I possibly can. I joined a theater company in Burbank, where I met slews of great people. Some of this is luck, some is connections. But again, some of this is just showing up, being as persistent as you can be. I keep showing up, making my little baby steps. Co-star roles will lead to bigger roles, and hopefully recurring roles, and one day I hope to have my own series. My dream is TV and more film, but I'm happy to do more commercials, theater work, and I can see happily making an income from my writing as well. I know that one's life can change dramatically in a day here—I've seen it happen. You never know.

I was so depressed and hopeless in the past. Honestly, I just started asking for help, and I got it. I finally could hear it. I had guidance from a higher power. People who came into my life were instrumental in my gaining hope, and they showed me that it wasn't all up to me. I saw that I could have faith in a higher power, a bigger picture. Previously, I had more faith in my abilities, my intellect, my own drive, what I could personally accomplish. Now, I can relax a little, and trust that it isn't all up to me.

People say I'm brave, but it doesn't feel like bravery. I received the answers in boldface, capital letters, like a sign with big lights all around it. I feel that kind of guidance is with me all the time now. When I get worried that a gig isn't coming, or I won't be able to pay the bills, it simply means I'm not connected enough. To feel better, I ask for help to connect to my higher power, and that's all I do. It always helps me. When I think I might want to pay somebody to look in a crystal ball and tell me the future, I stop, just make myself sit and be quiet, and I get the same info for free!

By following her heart, soul, and inner voice, Laura discovered that our dreams are possible, if we can figure out how to get out of our own way and show up every day investing all we can in them, without fail and without fear.

Sad to say, our contemporaries—our family, friends, colleagues, bosses, everyone who surrounds us—are often too filled with doubt, negativity, fear, and anxiety to support us on the path of following our soul's work. The vast majority of Americans (I believe the situation is different in other cultures) don't have a clue about the real "chops" required to do soul-fulfilling work. So how would they know what's possible and what's necessary? They don't. Our world today is more about outer achievements—money, houses, cars, technology, and gadgets. We're good at finding role models for winning these types of outer prizes. But where are the role models for doing soul-fulfilling work, loving it, and making a great living at it? They are rare indeed. In the absence of role models, you have a better source of guidance, a more reliable source that won't waver or let you down. This source is your inner voice, your higher self. This is the voice of your divine creative spirit, and it guides you to a more joyful, fulfilling life.

Laura says of her life now: *I'm in the best relationship I've ever had, and it's just getting better and better. My career is going baby step by baby step—I'm working my tail off, with great roles and really exciting projects coming. I'm doing exactly what I want to be doing, and I'm so happy. I've lost eighty pounds since 2001, when I was most depressed. My family sees how fulfilled I am, and even though I'm having only a modicum of success right now, they trust that I'm living the life that's right for me.*

Right now, my existence is not financially rich, but it's spiritually rich. I'm very resourceful and I'll be able to say, "Well, you know what, if when I'm 60 I have to go be a Wal-Mart greeter to pay the rent, at least I'll know that I gave 3,000 percent of what I could possibly put into this career." I would much rather live from that place than think, "Gosh, I have this corporate job, this big house, these cars, I get to vacation wherever I want, but if only I'd really tried to pursue my dream, I wonder where I could be." It's a choice I've consciously made.

My frustration is at how slowly the money comes. But I absolutely believe that financial prosperity will come to me from doing this work. I trust that if I just keep showing up as I am, giving it my committed and passionate all, each and every day, my life will be as I envision it. It's already happened. I'm happy, loved, healthy, and loving my life. What could be better?

LAURA'S ADVICE

- Relax, it's not all up to you. It's not all about your drive, your power, your abilities, your knowledge. Help and support much bigger and more powerful than what you're capable of on your own are available to you.
- Don't listen to others who say what you "should" do. Have trust, and reconcile making a living at doing what you can't live without doing.
- Ask for higher source help and get quiet to listen for the answer, then act on it, 3,000 percent.

Relax, It's Not All Up to You

Many of us were raised with the American ethic of personal achievement and the need to conquer. We were given the notion that it's up to each of us, individually and solely, to hack out the life we want, sometimes crushing others (and ourselves) to get it. After many years of struggle and despair, Laura discovered that her life wasn't all up to her. She found more powerful help—her belief in a higher power, a universal energy that connects her with herself and the world around her. This energy elevates her above her individual capabilities and knowledge. Laura accessed her higher power by going inward, listening quietly and patiently to hear her soul speaking. Others find their higher power through religion, spirituality, healing, energy work, meditation, praying, or serving others. I've found my connection to a higher power by casting off all of the rigid doctrine I was taught that felt false. I reconstructed a working concept of spirituality that feels right.

I believe in an all-loving universal energy that flows through and connects of us. Some call it God, others call it Love. Whatever you call it, if you connect with your higher power in a way that resonates for you, life changes. When you hear the sound of your own soul whispering to you, you'll know it in a second. There will be no doubt. You will be changed by the love, tolerance, lightness, optimism, and surety that you hear there, inside of you.

Reconcile Making a Living Doing What You Must

Each story in this book has reinforced that you need to stop resisting what you're compelled to do, and what you've come here to do. Whether it's singing, comedy, helping to reduce world poverty, speaking up for yourself, teaching children to love literature, overcoming abuse, or healing your body, women have found a way to do what they longed to do most—live their lives fully and passionately. These stories ask you to do the same—stop resisting what you are compelled to do. Embrace the very thing that you would give up everything for. Find the thing that makes you more than yourself, greater than you could be without it, and make it your *child*. Love it, nurture it, feed it, believe in it, and give to it as if your life depended on it, because it does.

Doing so is the surest way to overcome your crises and challenges. Find the courage and power to claim the life you long for. The rage and hopelessness that many women feel today, the quiet desperation of thousands on our planet, directly result from being thwarted. We are told we can't do what we wish to do. We believed that we were small. We felt cut off, struggling and alone on our journey.

We're not alone. And help is available. But to be helped, commit to being all that you dream to be. By taking steps to honor the reality of who you are, you gain what you need most—self-love, self-respect, and self-power. When you stand up to accept the life you're compelled toward, the world conspires to support you.

Get Higher Source Help

Laura's higher wisdom came to her on her thirty-minute train ride, in the form of a small inner voice that she could hear simply by being quiet and going within. People tap into their higher source help in many ways. Each method can be effective and life-changing. The key is to find the way that works best for you. What can you do to soothe the chatter of your mind, calm your worries, relax your body? Today, find a way to tap into your higher wisdom.

Here's how I access my inner guidance. Daily, if I can, I walk alone for thirty minutes in my neighborhood. No matter how agitated or frustrated I may be at the beginning of my walk, by the end, my worries have faded, my troubling questions have been answered, and I have clear next steps. For me, being in nature is therapeutic and purifying—the trees, grass, clouds, animals, the fresh breeze, the hawks circling in the air. I feel connected to everything. A sense of oneness and happiness takes me away from my momentary challenges and brings me a sense of power and peace.

I also write to what I call my "angels." Trudy Griswold, a wonderful spiritual coach, introduced me to this approach. Trudy is the coauthor of *Angelspeake*,[1] a lovely guidebook about communicating with angels. I discovered I could access my higher wisdom by sitting quietly at the computer with my eyes closed, relaxed and peaceful. After taking three deep cleansing breaths, I ask for help, and help always comes. Words appear in my mind, and I begin typing (much faster than usual, interestingly) as the answers to my questions stream out. The unique language I'm given, the outlook, the knowledge, and the sense of all-powerful love truly feel as if they are from another source or entity. What I write gives me a far broader perspective than I am capable of otherwise. Whether these are truly angels or spirit guides, or my tapping into a collective consciousness, or simply my imagination, the definition matters less to me than the fact that the information I receive, and the feeling that comes over me physically and emotionally as I receive it, have been of tremendous comfort and help. I receive precious gifts—new ideas, projects, questions to address, and suggested actions to take, and, most important, new ways to accept and believe in myself. I follow this guidance because it is always beneficial.

It doesn't matter whether you choose to meditate during your train commute, take walks, garden, do yoga, sit on the beach, rest in a sanctuary, or write to your angels. What's critical is that you find a way to quiet your mind, soothe your body, and tap into your vast inner knowledge and power, daily. But accessing it isn't enough. Once you hear your inner wisdom, follow it, and act boldly.

MOVING FORWARD TO BREAKTHROUGH

✳ STEP BACK

In your journal, capture all your thoughts. *No censoring, please—write everything that comes to mind.*

- What dreams for your life have gone unattended?
- *Who* specifically told you to give up on these dreams?

- Why did they advise you to give up on these dreams? What did they want to protect or keep you from?
- How has your life gone for you so far, not moving toward these dreams/visions?
- If you knew you simply couldn't fail, what would you be doing now in life and work?
- How would that situation be different from where you are today?

✳ LET GO of "shoulding."

- What "shoulds" have you been told by others throughout your life? Here are just a few common examples.

  I should:
  Put others' needs before my own
  Be responsible
  Give up childish dreams
  Be realistic
  Know my own limits
  Focus on security and making money
  Stop being childish
  Accept I'm not good enough to make it
  Do something practical with my career

- It's time to delete your "shoulds." Make a list of your "wants" instead. Here are some "wants" to explore.

  I want to:
  Put my needs first now
  Follow my dreams
  Believe I can do this
  Think very big
  Expand beyond my current limits
  Focus on having a life of passion, power, and purpose—a happy life
  Embrace my inner child
  Accept that I'm absolutely good enough!
  Do what I dream of with my career

- Whenever possible, shed actions that support "shoulds" in cases where they are a serious mismatch to your "wants."
- Take one step today toward making your "wants" a reality.

✳ SAY YES! to doing what you can't live without.

Recommended Steps

1. Try this exercise to access your inner, higher wisdom; you'll need your journal.

   Find a comfortable room to sit in quietly, with no interruptions, for fifteen minutes. Close your eyes and take three long, deep, cleansing breaths, each one deeper and more relaxing than the next.

   When you feel centered and at peace, begin to focus on going deep inside yourself, and ask, *"What can't I live without doing? What do I need to know or see that will help me embrace what I can't live without?"*

   Now wait. Listen quietly and carefully. Do not worry about anything. Put your mind at ease. What comes is what is meant to come.

   What do you see or hear? You may see images, like a small video clip in your mind, or you may hear words, or feel physical sensations. Write down everything you see, hear, and feel.

   Ask any burning question you have, and wait for the answer. There is no wrong way to do this. Whatever you receive is fine and as it should be. If you're not sure whether you see or hear anything specific, don't worry. In time, you will feel more comfortable in this process and begin to realize that you are indeed capable of tapping into information, guidance, and wisdom that is far above and beyond what you thought possible. All it takes is practice, commitment, and acceptance—saying yes.

   End with a moment of gratitude, a "thank you" to yourself for connecting with your higher dimension.

2. Once you have done this exercise, review all the information you received.

- What did it *feel* like to receive it? What physical sensations and emotions did you experience?
- What did the information suggest in terms of your life now and the changes you most desire?
- What did you learn that surprised you?
- What did this exercise tell you about the rightness of pursuing your dreams for your life and work?

3. Whatever you received, give thanks. If action is suggested, and if this action feels right, then take it.

4. Do something today that moves you forward toward what you can't live without.

Remember

Stop resisting what your life is compelled to be. Move toward doing what you cannot *not* do.

Laura reminds us

"There's a vast difference between living 'in the trenches' versus taking the time to see the 60,000-foot view and living from that perspective. For years, I was in the trenches, but I won't live like that a second longer. I realize that my soul's journey was to take the risk to get out of the trenches. It's so important to remember to stay connected to your higher power while working to fly high above the trenches. Sixty thousand feet up offers a far more beautiful view."

✳ **BREAKTHROUGH** "My work and play represent the real *Me*."

CONCLUSION

Claiming Your Passion, Power, and Purpose

The stories you've read here are all true. They haven't been enhanced to sound more compelling. They tell it like it was and is. These stories are inspiring not because of their uniqueness but because of their universality. Many women today are reclaiming their lives and finding passion, power, and purpose in the process. They are moving away from what's keeping them down, powerless, and stuck. Thousands of women are actively choosing to create a life of joy and fulfillment.

These women all have heart, guts, intuition, trust, and compassion for themselves and others. As I conducted research for this book and wrote *Breakdown, Breakthrough*, I discovered something surprising. This type of inspirational thinking, courage, and action can be found everywhere, if we open our eyes to see it. Wherever they are—in every Starbucks, on every soccer field, in the corporate ranks or in entrepreneurial circles, in creative think tanks or in local quilting classes—women of all walks of life, with all sorts of education and backgrounds, are changing, growing, stretching. They are reaching inward, as well as upward, to find themselves again.

While clearly it's challenging for women to balance what's on their plates, and do it on their terms, they're finding ways to do just that. Women are walking away from their fears, their resistance, and their wounds from the past to claim their power. Women who do are instrumental role models for others. And by following their dreams, and helping other women do the same, we ensure that outdated cultural patterns or career models will be revised, making room for more expansive, inclusive experiences for our daughters and granddaughters.

The one most important message to take away from this book is this: *If there is something that you would give up everything for, something that would make you feel sure about why you're on this planet now, and utterly joyful in it, then commit yourself to it.*

If you cannot *not* live a certain type of life, then go for it! Stop resisting it. Don't give up on your soul-felt dreams of what you want for your life. Keep them alive and dedicate yourself 3,000 percent to doing what's required to be what you want to be. Of course, there are no guarantees. The end point will most likely look very different from what you imagine. *But the journey toward the desired outcome is what's essential.*

What would happen if each of us stopped giving up on our dreams and committed to them full-throttle? Much of the rage and despair we feel and express would be healed. The world would change.

In reading this book, what have you come away with? What have learned about your journey and your challenges? What have you become aware of, in yourself, in others, in your situation, upbringing, and relationships, and in your dreams and visions? What will help you move forward today toward what you want most in life? And where will you find support to keep yourself aligned with those individuals and situations that encourage you to be all you wish to be?

If you are in breakdown mode, don't despair. You're not alone, and great help is available. For a start, see the Recommended Reading, Websites, and Groups list provided in the back of this book. Reach out to find a great coach or therapist. Ask a mentor to help. Enlist the support of a women's organization in your area to research a new direction or to help you fund it. Whatever resonates for you, do it. Remember, it's not all up to you, and you are powerful enough to succeed.

As new challenges emerge, review the recommendations in this book for support (for a summary, see the Empowerment Guide in the Resources section). If your family, friends, and colleagues also want to reclaim passion and power in their lives, please share this book with them, and consider forming your own **Breakdown, Breakthrough Circle**. There is strength in numbers, and breaking through is easier when you have ongoing empowering support to do it. For guidelines on starting your own **Breakdown, Breakthrough Circle**, please see www.elliacommunications.com.

As you take action, I hope you will assist others by relating stories of your progress on the blog for this book, at www.elliacommunications.com/blog. Please be generous and share with other women the insights you've gained and the progress you've made. There are no better teachers than those who themselves are claiming the life they dream of.

If you long for life change, now is the time to make it. In the end, there are no excuses. There is just action. I hope you are ready to take it.

As Leslie Morgan Steiner shared, despite the many challenges we women face in creating the lives we dream of, "I wouldn't trade living in this moment in history for anything." I couldn't agree more.

RESOURCES

I. EMPOWERMENT WITH SELF

CRISIS *Resolving Chronic Health Problems* (chapter 4)

✳ **STEP BACK TO EXPLORE** The body is communicating what the lips are not.

✳ **LET GO** of ignoring or resisting *what is.*

✳ **SAY YES!** to hearing your body, your intuition, and your heart.

✳ **BREAKTHROUGH** "I am healthy and strong."

✳ **BEST ADVICE** Hear your body. Heed your intuition. Follow your heart.

CRISIS *Overcoming Loss* (chapter 5)

✳ **STEP BACK TO EXPLORE** Grieving lost parts of yourself.

✳ **LET GO** of overidentifying with one aspect.

✳ **SAY YES!** to healing lost parts of yourself.

✳ **BREAKTHROUGH** "I am integrated and whole."

✳ **BEST ADVICE** Bring suppressed parts forward. Avoid overidentification. Find a "better way."

CRISIS *Achieving Self-Love* (chapter 6)

✳ **STEP BACK TO EXPLORE** Needing to reclaim your power from a source outside of you.

✳ **LET GO** of giving up your power to others or things.

✳ **SAY YES!** to acting in alignment with the *real* you.

✳ **BREAKTHROUGH** "I love and accept myself."

✳ **BEST ADVICE** Discover where you are being false. Find the power inside you. Disentagle from your struggle.

EMPOWERMENT GUIDE

II. EMPOWERMENT WITH OTHERS

CRISIS *Speaking Up with Power* (chapter 7)

✳ **STEP BACK TO EXPLORE** Reliving past trauma over speaking up.

✳ **LET GO** of your pain from past suppression.

✳ **SAY YES!** to your personal power through words and action.

✳ **BREAKTHROUGH** "I use my voice to support myself and others."

✳ **BEST ADVICE** Say what you want to say. Use positive language. Heal past suppression.

CRISIS *Breaking Cycles of Mistreatment* (chapter 8)

✳ **STEP BACK TO EXPLORE** Boundaries in need of strengthening.

✳ **LET GO** of your belief in your powerlessness.

✳ **SAY YES!** to developing healthy boundaries.

✳ **BREAKTHROUGH** "I am treated with love and respect."

✳ **BEST ADVICE** Develop healthy boundaries. Stop pleasing others to fill your needs. Get advocacy.

CRISIS *Shifting from Competition to Collaboration* (chapter 9)

✳ **STEP BACK TO EXPLORE** Feeling the need to prove your worth over and over.

✳ **LET GO** of feeling "not good enough."

✳ **SAY YES!** to your innate worthiness and value.

✳ **BREAKTHROUGH** "I am enough."

✳ **BEST ADVICE** Heal not feeling good enough. Look at the cost of "winning at all costs." Get real—you don't want to play this game.

III. EMPOWERMENT WITH THE WORLD

CRISIS *Escaping Financial Traps* (chapter 10)

✳ **STEP BACK TO EXPLORE** Valuing money above all else.

✳ **LET GO** of beliefs, relationships, and actions that keep you small.

✳ **SAY YES!** to a balanced relationship with money.

✳ **BREAKTHROUGH** "I fulfill my financial needs and honor who I am."

✳ **BEST ADVICE** Balance your money relationship. Know what you long to do and honor it. Shed what keeps you down.

CRISIS *Using Real Talents in Life and Work* (chapter 11)

✳ **STEP BACK TO EXPLORE** Denying the power of your unique gifts.

✳ **LET GO** of your fears of failure and inadequacy.

✳ **SAY YES!** to believing in your talents without fail.

✳ **BREAKTHROUGH** "I use my real talents in life and work."

✳ **BEST ADVICE** Know your natural talents. Get solid in your belief in yourself. Be open to angels in your life.

CRISIS *Helping Others and the World* (chapter 12)

✳ **STEP BACK TO EXPLORE** Resisting the fact that you can make a difference.

✳ **LET GO** of believing you don't have what it takes.

✳ **SAY YES!** to changing the world.

✳ **BREAKTHROUGH** "I help others and the world."

✳ **BEST ADVICE** Stop resisting your new path. Enjoy life's preciousness. Trust you can help the world.

IV. EMPOWERMENT WITH HIGHER SELF

CRISIS *Falling Together After Falling Apart* (chapter 13)

✳ **STEP BACK TO EXPLORE** A connection to struggle and to what no longer serves.

✳ **LET GO** of making excuses.

✳ **SAY YES!** to creating your new life as you want it.

✳ **BREAKTHROUGH** "I know what is important to me, and I honor it."

✳ **BEST ADVICE** Stop making excuses. Get someone to hold you accountable. Find a powerful role model.

CRISIS *Balancing Life and Work* (chapter 14)

✳ **STEP BACK TO EXPLORE** Overfunctioning and perfectionism to control your world.

✳ **LET GO** of your fears about not being in control.

✳ **SAY YES!** to being helped by others and your higher self.

✳ **BREAKTHROUGH** "I balance my life and work with joy."

✳ **BEST ADVICE** Stop overfunctioning. Address what you fear most. Get help from others and your higher self.

CRISIS *Doing Work and Play You Love* (chapter 15)

✳ **STEP BACK TO EXPLORE** Believing others who say you should let your dreams go.

✳ **LET GO** of "shoulding."

✳ **SAY YES!** to doing what you can't live without.

✳ **BREAKTHROUGH** "My work and play represent the real *Me*."

✳ **BEST ADVICE** Relax, it's not all up to you. Reconcile making a living doing what you must. Get higher source help.

Recommended Reading, Websites, and Groups

Books

Career

Hewlett, Sylvia Ann. *Off-Ramps and On-Ramps: Keeping Talented Women on the Road to Success.* Boston: Harvard Business School Press, 2007.

Ibarra, Herminia. *Working Identity: Unconventional Strategies for Reinventing Your Career.* Boston: Harvard Business School Press, 2003.

Jansen, Julie. *I Don't Know What I Want, But I Know It's Not This: A Step-by-Step Guide to Finding Gratifying Work.* New York: Penguin Books, 2003.

McKenna, Elizabeth Perle. *When Work Doesn't Work Anymore: Women, Work and Identity.* New York: Delta, 1998.

Wendleton, Kate. *Targeting a Great Career.* Clifton Park, NY: Thomson Delmar Learning, 2005.

Children and Teens

Carroll, Lee, and Jan Tober. *The Indigo Children: The New Kids Have Arrived.* Carlsbad, CA: Hay House, 1999.

Cohen-Sandler, Roni. *Stressed-Out Girls: Helping Them Thrive in the Age of Pressure.* New York: Viking / Penguin, 2005.

Coaching and Personal Development

Beck, Martha. *Finding Your Own North Star: Claiming the Life You Were Meant to Live.* New York: Three Rivers Press, 2001.

Blumenthal, Noah. *You're Addicted to You: Why It's So Hard to Change—And What You Can Do About It.* San Francisco: Berrett-Koehler Publishers, 2007.

Katie, Byron, and Stephen Mitchell. *Loving What Is: Four Questions That Can Change Your Life.* New York: Three Rivers Press, 2003.

Richardson, Cheryl. *Take Time for Your Life: A Personal Coach's Seven-Step Program for Creating the Life You Want.* New York: Broadway Books, 1999.

Creativity

Cameron, Julia. *The Artist's Way: A Spiritual Path to Higher Creativity.* New York: Tarcher / Putnam, 2002.

Grieving and Death

Kübler-Ross, Elisabeth. *On Death and Dying.* New York: Scribner, 1997.

Kübler-Ross, Elisabeth, and David Kessler. *On Grief and Grieving: Finding the Meaning of Grief Through the Five Stages of Loss.* New York: Scribner, 2007.

Healing

Hay, Louise L. *You Can Heal Your Life.* Carlsbad, CA: Hay House, 2004.

Myss, Caroline. *Anatomy of the Spirit: The Seven Stages of Power and Healing.* New York: Three Rivers Press, 1996.

Humor

Marvez, Monique. *Not Skinny, Not Blonde*: A Heartwrenching, Hilarious Memoir. For more details, see www.sandiegojack.com.

Life Experience

Boyle, Prill. *Defying Gravity: A Celebration of Late-Blooming Women.* Cincinnati: Emmis Books, 2005.

Love, Intimacy, and Marriage

Gottman, John M., and Nan Silver. *The Seven Principles for Making Marriage Work: A Practical Guide from the Country's Foremost Relationship Expert.* New York: Three Rivers Press, 1999.

Hendrix, Harville. *Getting the Love You Want: A Guide for Couples*, 20th anniversary edition. New York: Holt Paperbacks / Henry Holt and Co., 2008.

Jampolsky, Gerald G., Hugh Prather, and Jack O. Keeler. *Love Is Letting Go of Fear*. Berkeley, CA: Celestial Arts, 2004.

Schnarch, David. *Passionate Marriage: Love, Sex, and Intimacy in Emotionally Committed Relationships*. New York: W. W. Norton, 1997.

Meaning and Purpose

Frankl, Viktor E. *Man's Search for Meaning*. Boston: Beacon Press, 2006.

Meditation

Gawain, Shakti. *Creative Visualization Meditations*, 2nd edition. CD. Novato, CA: New World Library, 2002.

Gawain, Shakti. *Creative Visualization: Use the Power of Your Imagination to Create What You Want in Your Life*, 25th anniversary edition. Novato, CA: New World Library, 2002.

Goleman, Daniel. *The Meditative Mind*. New York: Tarcher / Putnam, 1996.

Midlife

Sheehy, Gail. *Passages: Predictable Crises of Adult Life*. New York: Bantam, 1977.

Shellenbarger, Susan. *The Breaking Point: How Today's Women Are Navigating Midlife Crisis*. New York: Henry Holt and Co., 2004.

Motherhood

Steiner, Leslie Morgan, ed. *Mommy Wars: Stay-at-Home and Career Moms Face Off on Their Choices, Their Lives and Their Families*. New York: Random House, 2007.

Parenting

Faber, Adele, and Elaine Mazlish. *How to Talk So Kids Will Listen and Listen So Kids Will Talk*. New York: Quill / HarperCollins, 2002.

Phelan, Thomas. *1-2-3 Magic: Effective Discipline for Children 2–12*. Glen Ellyn, IL: ParentMagic, Inc., 2004.

Richardson, Brenda Lane, and Elane Rehr. *101 Ways to Help Your Daughter Love Her Body*. New York: HarperCollins, 2001.

Prosperity and Finances

Bach, David. *Smart Women Finish Rich: Nine Steps to Achieving Financial Security and Funding Your Dreams*. New York: Broadway, 2002.

Eker, T. Harv. *Secrets of the Millionaire Mind: Mastering the Inner Game of Wealth*. New York: HarperCollins, 2005.

Nemeth, Maria. *The Energy of Money: A Spiritual Guide to Financial and Personal Fulfillment*. New York: Ballantine Wellspring, 1999.

Orman, Suze. *Women and Money: Owning the Power to Control Your Destiny*. New York: Spiegel & Grau, 2007.

Ponder, Catherine. *The Dynamic Laws of Prosperity*. Camarillo, CA: DeVorss Publications, 1962.

Ramsey, Dave. *The Total Money Makeover Workbook: A Proven Plan for Financial Success*. Nashville, TN: Thomas Nelson, 2003.

Psychology

Maslow, Abraham. *Toward a Psychology of Being*, 3rd edition. New York: Wiley, 1999.

Rogers, Carl. *A Way of Being*. New York: Houghton Mifflin Co., 1980.

Self-Image and Self-Esteem

Galler, Suzie. *I Am My Mother's Daughter*. DVD. Available from www.esteemedwoman.com.

Spirituality

Chopra, Deepak. *The Seven Spiritual Laws of Success: A Pocketbook Guide to Fulfilling Your Dreams*, abridged edition. San Rafael, CA: Amber-Allen Publishing, 2007.

Choquette, Sonia. *Your Heart's Desire: Instructions for Creating the Life You Really Want*. New York: Three Rivers Press, 2007.

Crum, Thomas. *Three Deep Breaths: Finding Power and Purpose in a Stressed-Out World*. San Francisco: Berrett-Koehler Publishers, 2006.

Dalai Lama and H. C. Cutler. *The Art of Happiness: A Handbook for Living*. New York: Riverhead Books / The Berkeley Publishing Group, 1998.

Dyer, Wayne. *Manifest Your Destiny: The Nine Spiritual Principles for Getting Everything You Want*. New York: HarperPaperbacks / HarperCollins, 1997.

Gawain, Shakti. *Developing Intuition: Practical Guidance for Daily Life*. Novato, CA: New World Library, 2000.

Hicks, Jerry, and Esther Hicks. *Ask and It Is Given: Learning to Manifest Your Desires.* Carlsbad, CA: Hay House, 2005.

Mark, Barbara, and Trudy Griswold. *Angelspeake, A Guide: How to Talk with Your Angels.* New York: Simon and Schuster, 1995.

Ruiz, Don Miguel. *The Four Agreements: A Practical Guide to Personal Freedom, A Toltec Wisdom Book.* San Rafael, CA: Amber-Allen Publishing, 1997.

Walsch, Neale Donald. *Conversations with God: An Uncommon Dialogue (Book 1).* New York: G. P. Putnam's Sons, 1996.

Wilkinson, Bruce. *The Prayer of Jabez: Breaking Through to the Blessed Life.* Sisters, OR: Multnomah Publishers, 2000.

Williamson, Marianne. *A Return to Love: Reflections on the Principles of "A Course in Miracles."* New York: HarperCollins, 1996.

Transitions

Bridges, William. *Transitions. Making Sense of Life's Changes*, 25th anniversary edition. Cambridge, MA: Da Capo Press / Perseus Books Group, 2004.

Websites and Groups

Breakdown, Breakthrough

www.breakdownbreakthrough.com
www.elliacommunications.com

Career

Business Plans
Bplans.com, www.bplans.com

Funding and Support
Ladies Who Launch, www.ladieswholaunch.com
Make Mine a Million Dollar Business, www.makeamillion.org

Job Search
Craigslist.com, www.craigslist.com
Hire Aspirations, www.hireaspirationsusa.com
HotJobs.com, www.hotjobs.com

Monster.com, www.monster.com

MyJobSearch.com, www.myjobsearch.com

Women @ Work Network, www.womenatwork.com

Planning Your Career

CareerJournal, *The Wall Street Journal*, www.careerjournal.com

CareerPerfect.com, www.careerperfect.com

CareerPlanner.com, www.careerplanner.com

Fast Company Magazine, www.fastcompany.com

Franchise.com, www.franchise.com

U.S. Small Business Administration, www.sba.gov

Coaching

International Coach Federation, www.coachfederation.org

Life Purpose Institute, www.lifepurposeinstitute.com

Institute for Life Coach Training, www.lifecoachtraining.com

Domestic Violence Prevention

U.S. Department of Health and Human Services, Center for Disease Control and
     Prevention, Domestic Violence Prevention, www.cdc.gov/ncipc/dvp/dvp.htm

National Coalition Against Domestic Violence, www.ncadv.org

Empowering Women

Esteemed Woman Foundation, www.esteemedwoman.com

Green Products and Living

Eco-Bags, www.ecobags.com

Loofah-Art, LLC, www.loofah-art.com

Patagonia, www.Patagonia.com

Recycline, www.recycline.com

Midlife

American Association of Retired Persons, www.aarp.com

Gen Plus+, www.genplususa.com

More Magazine, www.moremagazine.com

National Association of Baby Boomer Women, www.nabbw.com

Motherhood
The Momference, www.momference.com

Nonprofits
American Red Cross, www.redcross.org
The Blessing Basket Project®, www.blessingbasket.org
Habitat for Humanity, www.habitat.org

Psychotherapy
American Association of Marriage and Family Therapy, www.aamft.org

Spirituality
Abraham-Hicks, www.abraham-hicks.com
Angelspeake, www.angelspeake.com
Astrology Zone by Susan Miller, www.astrologyzone.com
Shakti Gawain, www.shaktigawain.com
The International Center for Reiki Training, www.reiki.org
Neal Donald Walsch, www.cwg.org/main.php

Sustainable Development
Mountain Forum, www.mtnforum.org

Working Women
Catalyst, www.catalyst.org
Working Mother Magazine, www.workingmother.com

Workplace Issues
Center for Work-Life Policy, www.worklifepolicy.org
Families and Work Institute, www.familiesandwork.org
U.S. Department of Labor, Family and Medical Leave Act,www.dol.gov/esa/whd/fmla
U.S. Equal Opportunity Employment Commission, www.eeoc.gov

World Music
Arthur Lipner, www.arthurlipner.com

NOTES

Introduction: The Power of Yes!

1. *Merriam-Webster OnLine Dictionary*, www.m-w.com/dictionary/crisis.

1. Breakdown in Professional Women—Why Now?

1. In 2007, women made up 46.4 percent of the labor force and 50.6 percent of managerial, professional, and related positions. Of all women over 16, 59.3 percent were in the labor force, compared to 73.2 percent of all men. In 2006, 53.8 percent of all mothers with children under 1 were in the labor force. The overall labor force participation rate of parents with children under 18 in 2006 was 70.9 percent for mothers and 94.1 percent for fathers. And in 2007, 15.4 percent of Fortune 500 corporate officer positions were held by women, down from 15.6 percent in 2006. Catalyst, "Statistical Overview of Women in the Workplace" Quick Takes, April 2008; www.catalyst.org/publication/219/statistical-overview-of-women-in-the-workplace.

2. Between 1990 and 2005, women's median income grew 31.6 percent ($14,112 to $18,576), compared to 10.0 percent for men ($28,439 to $31,275). In the United States in 2005, 25.5 percent of wives in dual-working couples earned more than their husbands. Women currently earn more bachelor's (57.5 percent) and master's degrees (60.0 percent) than men, and by 2016–17 are projected to continue to grow their share to earn more degrees than men in bachelor's (59.9 percent), master's (62.9 percent), doctorate (55.5 percent), and other professional degrees (53.3 percent). Catalyst, "Buying Power" Quick Takes, May 2008; www.catalyst.org/publication/256/buying-power.

3. Women's inflation-adjusted full-time earnings have risen 16.8 percent in the past fifteen years. Men's comparable earnings have declined 1.7 percent for the same period. Nearly one-third of wives now outearn their husbands, and the proportion of women earning more than $100,000 tripled in the past decade. Sue Shellenbarger, "The Female Midlife Crisis: More Women Than Men Now Report Upheaval by Age 50; The ATV Tipping Point," *The Wall Street Journal Online*, April 7, 2005; online.wsj.com/article/SB111283464791500330.html.

4. Diane F. Halpern, "APA Presidential Address: Psychology at the Intersection of Work and Family: Recommendations for Employers, Working Families, and Policymakers," *American Psychologist* 60, no. 5 (July–August 2005): 397–409.

5. "Women feel more overworked than men. At first, this finding seems counterintuitive since men tend to work longer hours, are more accessible to their employers during non-work time, are less likely to use all their vacation, and are more likely to have jobs with other characteristics that appear to contribute to feeling overworked than do women. In two important respects, however, women do report having more demanding jobs: On average, they report being interrupted more frequently while working and having too many tasks to do at the same time.

   "This finding raises important questions: Do women experience more frequent interruptions and too much multi-tasking because of the specific types of jobs they have? Do the socialization experiences of women make them more vulnerable to interruptions and more likely to take on additional tasks?" Ellen Galinsky, Stacy S. Kim, & James T. Bond, *Feeling Overworked: When Work Becomes Too Much* (New York: Families and Work Institute, 2001), 9–10.

6. Sylvia Ann Hewlett, *Off-Ramps and On-Ramps: Keeping Talented Women on the Road to Success* (Boston: Harvard Business School Press, 2007).

7. Susan Shellenbarger, *The Breaking Point: How Today's Women Are Navigating Midlife Crisis* (New York: Henry Holt and Co., 2004).

8. Elizabeth Enright, "A House Divided," *AARP Magazine*, July–August 2004; www.aarp magazine.org/family/Articles/a2004-05-26-mag-divorce.html.

2. Recognizing When You're in Professional Crisis

1. Roni Cohen-Sandler, *Stressed-Out Girls: Helping Them Thrive in the Age of Pressure* (New York: Viking / Penguin Group, 2005).

3. A New Model for Empowered Living

1. Abraham Maslow, *Toward a Psychology of Being*, 3rd ed. (New York: Wiley, 1999).

4. Resolving Chronic Health Problems

1. Louise L. Hay, *You Can Heal Your Life* (Carlsbad, CA: Hay House, 2004).

2. Shakti Gawain, *Creative Visualization Meditations*, CD, 2nd ed. (Novato, CA: New World Library, 2002).

3. Shakti Gawain, *Developing Intuition*, 2nd ed. (Novato, CA: New World Library, 2008).

4. Thomas Crum, *Three Deep Breaths: Finding Power and Purpose in a Stressed-Out World* (San Francisco: Berrett-Koehler Publishers, 2006).

5. Overcoming Loss

1. Read more about Mike Jaffe's story at www.jaffelifedesign.com.

7. Speaking Up with Power

1. Carl Rogers, *A Way of Being* (New York: Houghton Mifflin Company, 1980).
2. Don Miguel Ruiz, *The Four Agreements: A Practical Guide to Personal Freedom, A Toltec Wisdom Book* (San Rafael, CA: Amber-Allen Publishing, 1997).

10. Escaping Financial Traps

1. Maria Nemeth, *The Energy of Money: A Spiritual Guide to Financial and Personal Fulfillment* (New York: Ballantine Wellspring, 1999).

11. Using Real Talents in Life and Work

1. Monique Marvez, *Not Skinny, Not Blonde: A Heartwrenching, Hilarious Memoir.* For more details, see www.sandiegojack.com.

12. Helping Others and the World

1. Adapted from the Life Purpose Institute's Coach Certification Program (www.life purposeinstitute.com).

13. Falling Together After Falling Apart

1. The Blessing Basket Project®, www.blessingbasket.org.

14. Balancing Life and Work

1. Leslie Morgan Steiner, ed., *Mommy Wars: Stay-at-Home and Career Moms Face Off on Their Choices, Their Lives and Their Families* (New York: Random House, 2007).
2. Neale Donald Walsch, *Conversations with God: An Uncommon Dialogue (Book 1)* (New York: G. P. Putnam's Sons, 1995).

15. Doing Work and Play You Love

1. Barbara Mark and Trudy Griswold, *Angelspeake, A Guide: How to Talk with Your Angels* (New York: Simon and Schuster, 1995).

ACKNOWLEDGMENTS

I am deeply grateful to the many individuals who helped this book become a reality, and who supported and encouraged me all along the way.

My heartfelt gratitude goes out:

To Steve Piersanti and Johanna Vondeling of Berrett-Koehler—for believing in me and in this project, and for trusting in the future expansive vision of both.

To my wonderful BK editor, Johanna Vondeling—for your brilliant vision, clarity, and expertise. Thank you for your continual guidance, and for teaching me—with your kind and caring ways—the many first-time author lessons I needed to learn. This book would not exist without you.

To the entire Berrett-Koehler staff—for your tremendous talents and dedication. Thank you for the collaborative and immensely enriching author experience you foster.

To my readers, Kendra Armer, Carol Cartaino, Kathleen Epperson, and Kate Marshall—for your very instructive and motivating editorial feedback.

To Noah Blumenthal—for your generosity in connecting me with BK, and for your invaluable mentorship all along the way.

To my hundreds of research study and seminar participants, and my twelve featured interviewees—for your openness and generosity in sharing your fantastic stories of reinvention. I am inspired by your courage and power.

To my many therapy and coaching clients—who've shown me what it means to walk away from fear toward hope and strength.

To Suzie Galler—for launching me on my way as a speaker and author.

To Krista Reiner Carnes—for your tremendous development talents, and for helping me see what's possible in myself, and trust it.

To Janet Goldstein—for urging me to stretch bigger, and to marry holistically who I am with where I wish to go.

To my dearest Anne, Beth, and Lisa—for supporting me unfailingly as loving mentors, advocates, and friends—through all the bumps and triumphs.

To my spiritual friends, Beverly and Trudy—for helping me believe in my dreams and connect me to my intuition, my angels, and my highest self.

To my friend Mike Jaffe—for being my "gentle fire," waking me up and pushing me forward.

To my sister-in-law, Mara Lipner—for your love, humor, and generosity.

To Will Lippincott—for encouraging this new author with a big dream.

To my parents, Joseph and Georgia Caprino, for your lifelong encouragement and love.

To my beloved husband, Arthur Lipner—for who you are, and for your love and support—in this and all things. Thank you for sharing your soulful creativity, invincible spirit, and amazing gifts of love and inspiration.

To my dearest children—Julia and Elliot—for changing my life. Thank you for teaching me every day the *real* meaning of joy, creativity, and love.

INDEX

Other *Breakdown, Breakthrough* products available:

Breakdown, Breakthrough Study Guide for Groups (downloadable format)
Breakdown, Breakthrough Meditations and Exercises, audio CD
Breakdown, Breakthrough Journal

To order, visit The Ellia Store at www.elliacommunications.com/ellia-store.html

Book blog: www.elliacommunications.com/blog

To contact Kathy:
Kathy Caprino
Ellia Communications, Inc.
P.O. Box 302
Wilton, CT 06897
Email: kathy@elliacommunications.com
Web: www.elliacommunications.com

ABOUT THE AUTHOR

Kathy Caprino, MA, is an executive and life coach and a career transition consultant with more than eighteen years of professional experience leading staff and launching major business initiatives. A recognized expert in professional women's empowerment, she specializes in helping women gain power and self-mastery, and navigate successfully through transition to reclaim their lives.

She is president and founder of Ellia Communications, Inc., and former co-founder of Living in Harmony—The Center for Emotional Health, in Connecticut. She is an active member in the International Coach Federation and has her own private coaching practice. She also serves as a career transition consultant for Women@Work Network, LLC, in Connecticut.

Trained as a coach and a psychotherapist, Ms. Caprino has developed cutting-edge tools and approaches that help individuals move forward both emotionally and behaviorally. Important findings from her national in-depth research study, *Women Overcoming Professional Crisis: Finding New Meaning in Life and Work*, co-sponsored by the Esteemed Woman Foundation, led her to develop her new coaching Model for Empowered Living.

Ms. Caprino draws on her research, high-level corporate experience, training with families and systems, and coaching work with hundreds of midlife professionals to provide effective programs that help clients achieve desired growth in all areas of life.

Ms. Caprino is a vibrant, engaging speaker who delivers interactive seminars and talks for corporations and women's organizations at the local, regional, and national levels. Additional information about her coaching and speaking services is available at www.ellia communications.com. More information about *Breakdown, Breakthrough* can be found at www.breakdownbreakthrough.com.

An active vocalist and performer, Ms. Caprino lives in Connecticut with her husband, the renowned jazz percussionist Arthur Lipner (www.arthurlipner.com), their two beloved children, and two dogs.

✳

PRODUCED BY WILSTED & TAYLOR PUBLISHING SERVICES

PRODUCTION MANAGEMENT   *Christine Taylor*

PRODUCTION ASSISTANCE   *Drew Patty*

COPYEDITING   *Melody Lacina*

DESIGN AND COMPOSITION   *Yvonne Tsang*

PROOFREADING AND INDEXING   *Andrew Joron*

PRINTER'S BEDEVILMENT   *Lillian Marie Wilsted*

PRINTING AND BINDING   *Malloy Incorporated*

✳

About Berrett-Koehler Publishers

Berrett-Koehler is an independent publisher dedicated to an ambitious mission: Creating a World that Works for All.

We believe that to truly create a better world, action is needed at all levels—individual, organizational, and societal. At the individual level, our publications help people align their lives with their values and with their aspirations for a better world. At the organizational level, our publications promote progressive leadership and management practices, socially responsible approaches to business, and humane and effective organizations. At the societal level, our publications advance social and economic justice, shared prosperity, sustainability, and new solutions to national and global issues.

A major theme of our publications is "Opening Up New Space." They challenge conventional thinking, introduce new ideas, and foster positive change. Their common quest is changing the underlying beliefs, mindsets, and structures that keep generating the same cycles of problems, no matter who our leaders are or what improvement programs we adopt.

We strive to practice what we preach—to operate our publishing company in line with the ideas in our books. At the core of our approach is *stewardship*, which we define as a deep sense of responsibility to administer the company for the benefit of all of our "stakeholder" groups: authors, customers, employees, investors, service providers, and the communities and environment around us.

We are grateful to the thousands of readers, authors, and other friends of the company who consider themselves to be part of the "BK Community." We hope that you, too, will join us in our mission.

A BK Life Book

This book is part of our BK Life series. BK Life books change people's lives. They help individuals improve their lives in ways that are beneficial for the families, organizations, communities, nations, and world in which they live and work. To find out more, visit www.bk-life .com.

Visit Our Website

Go to www.bkconnection.com to read exclusive previews and excerpts of new books, find detailed information on all Berrett-Koehler titles and authors, browse subject-area libraries of books, and get special discounts.

Subscribe to our Free E-Newsletter

Be the first to hear about new publications, special discount offers, exclusive articles, news about bestsellers, and more! Get on the list for our free e-newsletter by going to www.bk connection.com.

Get Quantity Discounts

Berrett-Koehler books are available at quantity discounts for orders of ten or more copies. Please call us toll-free at (800) 929-2929 or email us at bkp.orders@aidcvt.cm.

Host a Reading Group

For tips on how to form and carry on a book reading group in your workplace or community, see our website at www.bkconnection.com.

Join the BK Community

Thousands of readers of our books have become part of the "BK Community" by participating in events featuring our authors, reviewing draft manucripts of forthcoming books, spreading the word about their favorite books, and supporting our publishing program in other ways. If you would like to join the BK Community, please contact us at bkcommunity@bkpub.com.